WESTERN HORSEMANSHIP

Charles R. Self, Jr.

WESTERN HORSEMANSHIP

Charles R. Self, Jr.

Winchester Press

Copyright © 1979 by Charles R. Self, Jr.

LIBRARY OF CONGRESS CATALOGING IN PUBLICATION DATA
Self, Charles R
    Western horsemanship.

    Includes index.
    1. Western riding.
    I. Title.
SF309.3.S44   798'.23   79-14535
ISBN 0-87691-291-9

9 8 7 6 5 4 3 2 1

Published by Winchester Press
205 East 42nd Street
New York, N.Y. 10017

WINCHESTER is a Trademark of Olin Corporation used by Winchester
Press, Inc. under authority and control of the Trademark Proprietor.

Printed in the United States of America

CONTENTS

FOREWORD

As any book takes its final shape, the writer has to begin to think of just how much credit is due him in the overall construction of the manuscript. Certainly the words and form are his, but the information comes from many sources, beginning with experience and moving on to people and groups and companies. I doubt many of the books I've written would have reached my editors without the assistance of a great many others.

In the case of *Western Horsemanship*, thanks have to go to an even longer list than usual, with special credit going to Tony Crilley and Jim Shands. Jodi and Virginia Crilley provided much aid in preparing horses for photography. Washington Manufacturing Company was gracious enough to supply our jacket photograph, and some shirts and jeans for our models, while Levi Strauss also supplied jeans. Charles Duff, chairman of Farnam Companies, was generous with grooming equipment for use in illustrations. Other aid came from the American Quarter Horse Association, the American Horse Show Association, the Appaloosa Horse Club, American Saddlery, Crafters, the Poron Division of Rogers Corporation, 3M, Shell Chemical Company, Tex Tan and others, including the people who put together the 4H horse program. Dr. Arden Huff, horse specialist for the extension division at VPI & SU, Blacksburg, Virginia, provided invaluable information.

More special thanks go to Doug Meador, trainer for L'Avenier Ranch, in Lynchburg, Virginia, for making available his time and riding ability and for locating the proper horse.

In addition, I am grateful to Sandra Shands for her patience in coping with my hand-scribbled corrections and typing the manuscript.

Hamley's and Fallis Saddlery helped in providing different points of view in saddle design.

To y'all, and those I overlooked, thanks.

INTRODUCTION

We've titled this book *Western Horsemanship* even though a good portion of the material will emphasize riding, a single aspect of horsemanship and a skill that does not always demonstrate total horsemanship. Though the cases are seldom, I've seen some really superb riders who are abominable horsemen. On the other hand, in a very few cases, an exceptional horseman may be a relatively poor rider—though that is a difficult decision to make because horsemanship is a totality, whether the riding and tack style be English or Western.

Horsemanship involves everything touching on your horse and its care, from your setting the saddle properly to sitting the saddle correctly to handling the hooves properly. In addition, the good horseman will also be sensitive to the horse at all times, so that the relationship between rider and animal is a comfortable one.

Another point and one quickly made: in referring to horsemanship, I include all humans who are involved with horses, male or female. No gender designation is intended, with horseman used in the same sense as is "mankind," to denote everyone. No reasonable term has yet been settled on to provide an overall term that doesn't suffer from extreme linguistic clumsiness, so we'll stick with the historic and customary at this time.

Horse care, thus horsemanship, is of extreme importance in the day-to-day enjoyment of your horse. An old saying, "Rode hard and put up wet," expresses it well, for the words are often used to describe people and animals who look much the worse for wear and lack of care. Horses treated in such a way will rapidly show signs of deterioration, probably more quickly than most other animals.

Horses are timid animals, and we must take this into consideration when working with them. Their entire history is that of animals conditioned to flee from danger, with fighting reserved to their own kind at mating times, or as a last resort. In fact, it is totally unnatural for a horse to accept a rider, or any other burden, on its back: the back is the spot where most equine predators prefer to land, so any weight in this area comes as a psychological threat to the horse.

For this reason, patience and time are one's best allies when training a horse. You must take care that while becoming accustomed to bearing the burden, the horse doesn't become so terrorized it becomes mean, overtimid, or develop any of dozens of other negative characteristics.

Once we begin to understand the workings of a horse's mind—as much as possible in light of the poor research to date—the relationship starts to be that of horseman and horse, rather than horse and rider, or some other, less pleasant combination.

Too, we must realize that any generalization—such as saying horses are timid and flee from their enemies—will have exceptions. There are a few—very few—horses who attack instead of fleeing. In any case, each horse is an individual and should be treated as such, with the horseman working to determine the level of intelligence, the athletic ability, and other qualities of his own animal.

Equine intelligence is a subject of some controversy, and will be until correct tests are devised. In a sense, horses are rather like culturally deprived children when it comes to IQ testing. The tests applied are those developed for canines and felines, or for various monkeys, animals with no psychological relationship to the horse. The first two are predators, while the monkey clan is closely akin to man in many ways and little related to equines. If a dog does such and such under a certain stimulus, he's considered a bright animal. If a horse reacts differently, he's stupid. Not necessarily. If you threaten a dog, and it returns the threat by swelling its ruff and snarling, that's to be expected. If you threaten an unrestrained horse, and he flees, that should be an indication of his intelligence, but too many people interpret flight as a stupid reaction because the animal's backside is then turned to the enemy, or predator—even though that backside can be formidable.

In any case, until enough equine psychological research is done to provide better answers, each of us will have to work from our own experiences to develop ideas for the handling of each horse, based on a few well-observed facts. Until we are sure of the questions, there is simply no way to get answers.

From this point comes the divergence and diversity of training methods today. Controversy is a norm among trainers, with one sneering at another daily, no matter what the results. Unless outright cruelty is involved, most modern horse-training methods can be made to work, but I would think that for the best results horsemen should emphasize one factor more than anything else: flexibility. Once you're beyond the basics, whether it is in riding or training, you'll need to formulate your own techniques, those things that work for you with a particular horse. The deciding factor shouldn't be whether it works for me, my friends, or anyone else. It must work for you and your horse to be of any value. What works for me may simply be because of the way I relate to a particular horse. Such an idea might provide only a base for you, or it might provide nothing. Stay loose and keep calm, and try to adapt to your animal. Adapt and become a horseman. Don't adapt and stay a rider.

Adaptability holds true all the way through training a horse, and continues to be of utmost importance in care and riding. You have to adapt because, in many ways, your horse can't. The basics of horse training, all well known, can bring on controversy. Fortunately, this book need not cover them, for a short while ago one of the West Coast's top trainers, Anthony Amaral (*How to Train Your Horse*, Winchester Press, 1977), did an excellent job on the subject.

This leaves one field: Western riding, both for pleasure and show. It is a single field that can cover everything from barrel racing to riding the hills of Virginia, Arizona, Oregon, New York, or anywhere. The sport has become so popular that a few rodeo cowboys have come here from areas as far away as France—and done rather well. There are riding clubs in many areas of Europe that specialize in Western-style riding.

The basics of Western riding relate to covering ground comfortably over moderately long periods of time. I have one friend who has had to spend as long as sixteen hours in the saddle for several days running—working cattle in land that God forgot (and doesn't want to be reminded of). Roping and cutting steers are elements of Western riding, for they're cowboys' work, and Western riding was developed by the nineteenth-century cowboy, with more than a little assistance from Spanish and Mexican riders of the same and the preceding century.

Different areas of the country saw different forms of Western saddle-rigging develop, as the terrain required, while differing cultural values gave rise to different training methods and different riding styles.

The hackamores, bosals, and spade bits of the Californios are still used in West Coast areas, and some East Coast trainers and riders prefer them, though overall they are used less frequently here. Old-timers tend to prefer them, along with the final result, the spade bit for the trained horse. Too often, the spade bit is thought of as an instrument of torture. It's not, if used as it is meant to be used. The California horse is brought along on bosal and hackamore, and then, when trained, switched to the spade bit. Its mouth is very soft and the lightest pressure on the reins brings an instant response. The mouth has never been used (hackamores and bosals use the pressure points on and around the muzzle to train a horse), and it is not hard in any way. For proper use of a spade bit, the rider must be as expert as his horse. Hard hands with a spade bit will ruin a horse's mouth in short order.

A spade bit, correctly used, provides widespread and even pressure in the mouth, and can thus often be more gentle than would be one of the less severe-looking grazing bits. Any bit in the hands of a clod is an instrument of torture and can cause soreness, callus, and a great deal of other damage to the horse's mouth.

Because of the damage a bit can do—a hackamore or bosal can also cause a fair amount of pain if incorrectly used—a lot of emphasis in this book will be placed on the rider developing soft hands. Soft hands are nothing more than hands that can feel a horse's headset and mouth with almost no pressure on the reins. Soft hands need do little more than provide gentle rein movement for control and a really good horseman is able to actually get more out of a horse because the hands help (along with the other aids and cues, as we'll see later on).

It should also be remembered that most Western horses are trained to neck rein, and that no actual mouth pressure, or very, very little, should be needed for directional changes. The only time even mild pressure is used on a horse is to stop or back it (and most times even that shouldn't be necessary). Some Western horses stop so immediately that a novice may spend more than a little time with one fist wrapped around the saddle horn to keep from flying over the horse's head.

Recently, Colonel A. H. Wilson, USA (retired), one of America's finest polo players, told me a tale of one of his rides that easily illustrates the speed with which such a horse can stop. Colonel Wilson was playing polo on a horse he later discovered had been trained for calf- and steer-roping events. Polo is a game that demands a horse put up with a rider clambering all over him, among other things, and Colonel Wilson, in preparation for a shot, placed his hand just forward of the saddle on the left-side withers. The stop that resulted catapulted this expert rider over the head of his horse. That particular spot is one that is favored when a roper trains his horse to stop once a steer has been heeled or headed so that the roped animal comes up against a taut rope.

Such training requires a great deal of time, and removing such training may require even more time. Knowing that a horse has been trained in such a way can be a help in holding onto one's seat, even with the greater support of a Western saddle over the European styles used in polo. (Roping saddles have slick forks so that the rider can dismount quickly, but then, the rider *knows* his horse is going to stop, and will usually be swinging out of the leather as the horse sets up to stop. Cutting saddles have more fork swell, for a cutting horse changes directions at a pace that would unseat most people easily: this is one contest event where you'll see even the best riders with one hand on the saddle horn almost all the time!)

Getting on a horse and plodding down the road, across a field, or over a trail isn't all that hard. If it were, most of the rental stables in the world would be out of business. But such riding doesn't provide much of the fun of true horsemanship,

Fig. 1. Doug Meador shows how a horse can set up and forget the methods after not being ridden for six weeks or so.

Fig. 2. A few minutes of work show the horse recalling proper foot position.

which, basically, requires not much more in the way of truly difficult thought or work, simply more saddle time, and much, much, more time around and handling horses.

A horse is a large animal compared to a human, and, as such, may intimidate those not familiar with him. Oddly enough, that huge animal is more easily intimidated than most humans could ever be—a flicker of light from a tin can by the side of the road; a startled bird flying close to its head; a sudden gust of wind whirling some dust around. Just about any such sudden event can startle a horse, and the events will often include things that seem nothing more than the horse's imagination.

Such intimidation is often dangerous—and a good trail horse must be trained not to shy or bolt because of such things—but the factors behind this ease of intimidation work for us in

making a horse do our bidding. Any horseman intimidates a
horse. That is essential. The horse must know you are its
master—many will test you every time you mount, while others
will test once and give up, and others may never test you.
Intimidation in this sense must not be equated with total fear.
A terrified horse is dangerous to itself and just about everything or anybody around. It will flee, with or without a rider on
its back. If cornered, it may well strike out with teeth and
hooves.

Intimidation, because of the connotation of fear attached, is
probably a poor word to use here, but essentially all we're
really doing is letting the horse know it is not its own master,
that it must do what you want it to do. And you can't do that by
physical power. Even a small horse is much larger than a
person, and larger horses are exceptionally powerful. For example, recently I was feeding a friend's mare and her filly, both
Thoroughbreds. If the mare didn't wish to be led to pasture,
she'd simply yank the lead rope from my hand. My friend's
children led this 16-2 mare around with a towel around her
neck. I tried that the first day. She is a large horse, possibly
1,200 pounds, but, then, I weigh 200 pounds or a bit more,
depending on my exercise time. She simply lifted me from my
feet and walked off to begin grazing around the barn. I let go of
the towel, snarled a bit, and then changed my voice tone. She
went into the pasture without any trouble. It was all in one's
tone of voice: the scene, in one variation or another, was repeated during the time I fed her. She was an independent
horse, but one that reacts properly when she feels that patience
has run out. In other words, I had to intimidate her before
she'd make the proper move.

Then again, horses react differently to different people. The
same pasture that held the mare holds Teamwork, a Thoroughbred gelding, and my friend's children often ride the animal
bareback and with English tack most of the rest of the time.
Teamwork is not trained to neck rein, but is a calm horse,
though the children sometimes have a bit of trouble making
him go.

Fig. 3. Dividend is ready to go. Jodi Crilley's Thoroughbred mare is an all-purpose horse, working well in English or Western and is a good hunter-jumper, too.

I dropped my Western rig on him a few weeks ago, though I kept the English bridle, with my reins attached (using a D-ring snaffle bit, as usual). Teamwork went, and he went well, at a walk and at a trot. I was a bit afraid my saddle, with Quarter Horse bars, wasn't right for the high-withered Thoroughbred, so I didn't ride long or fast. Oddly enough, I had to circle the horse to get him to stop. He went better for me than he had for the children, but wouldn't stop! The children had trouble getting him going and no trouble stopping. The gelding's owner had no trouble in either direction. The horse went and stopped well. (Here, though, we run into a classification that needs to be made: if I live to be 117, I will not ride as well as my friend, nor will many other people. A horse knows this, or discovers it in a very few minutes.)

Basically, then, each horse is an individual, though horses have many common traits. Recognizing the common traits requires some time, but recognizing and working with the individual traits is even harder and takes even more time and experience. It is up to each horseman to get to know a particular animal's quirks, and then apply the best methods for both horse and horseman. That's what horsemanship is all about.

With a bit of luck, and a lot of practice, this book will provide you with the basic information needed for you to become a horseman: not a horse trainer, but a horseman. There is not a chance it will make you a better horseman, or even a better rider, unless practice is added in large and frequent doses. You cannot become a good horseman by reading about horses, though some details are much more readily available that way.

Read and then go out and adapt and apply what you have read. If you really enjoy horses, you'll enjoy them more, and get much more from the experience.

CHARLES R. SELF JR.
Stone Mountain, Virginia

1. WESTERN RIDING STYLES

The Western horseman has so many kinds of games and territory to cover, whether in shows or just for fun, that a complete chapter is necessary to cover most of them. Even as this book is being written, we can bet someone is developing another contest, or a different kind of trail ride, so a thorough listing is difficult if not impossible. Some Western riding styles are easy and suitable for just about anyone at all, while others are dangerous even for experts who take part in them frequently. Some, though not dangerous, require years of practice and training. Games, timed events, Western pleasure-riding classes, a ride over the mountains, a camping trip; in short, almost anything you wish to do can be done on horseback, with experience and a bit of care.

The various rodeo events are well known to most people, and are somewhat out of place in a book on basic Western horsemanship as they tend to be very specialized and extremely rough on the body. Joe Alexander, featured on our book jacket, is a national rodeo champion and has been the national bareback-riding champion seven times. The styles and techniques he uses in the arena are totally different from those he uses on his ranch and for pleasure riding. There is a certain relationship between saddle bronc riding and the old-time skills used in breaking horses, but today's horses are seldom broken, or trained, in the same manner. Contemporary buckers are specially chosen and are very valuable horses with a natural tendency to buck. That tendency is intensified by use of a strap that puts just enough pressure on the horse's belly and kidney area to make it uncomfortable. Incidentally, many people think bucking horses are tortured into bucking because they stop as soon as the rider flies off or the strap is loosened. But in one case, the horse gets rid of an irritant—the rider—and stops; in the other, it gets rid of an even milder irritant, the strap, and stops, with little or no damage to either rider or horse—(if the rider's lucky; bucking horses in their mid-twenties are not uncommon, while rodeo riders in good shape at a comparable human age are definitely uncommon).

Fig. 4. The cutting horse and rider at work. Credit: Dalco and the American Quarter Horse Association.

Fig. 5. The cutting cowhorse has to be able to move at extreme angles. Credit: Leroy Weathers & AQHA.

Perhaps cutting is the rodeo event that looks easiest to the spectators, with the rider and his horse having to cut out and move into a chute several calves or steers in the specified time or less. But horses have what is known as cow savvy in different degrees, so that a horse that might be ideally suited, physically, to the competition, may be mentally unsuited. Months, even years, of training are required, and the horseman must be a total expert at anticipating the way a horse will go, for if the rider over or underbalances, the horse will feel the interference—this is one of several events where the horse actually has more control over what happens than does the rider—and lose time. Some riders have said that winning a cutting-horse event requires only a rider who has sense and skill enough to let the horse do what needs to be done. While this is an exaggeration, the horse is of exceptional importance in this event, and as a

Fig. 6. Single rope, calf roping. Credit: Dalco & AQHA.

Fig. 7. Heading and heeling, a far from easy pursuit. Credit: Alfred Janssen III & AQHA.

spectator, you will enjoy the spectacle more if you learn to appreciate the fine points involved—for example, the ways a horse picks up a cow and works with it.

Roping steers is an event where the horse has almost the same importance as it does in cutting. Cowboys will often lend a good roping horse to one another, with several people at the same rodeo roping with the best horse they're able to borrow. Much depends on the horse getting the rider to the correct spot as quickly as possible, with as little guidance from the rider as possible, and a good roping horse is often the difference between winning and losing, no matter how skilled the rider is. Still, roping itself is an art that needs constant practice, and until you've handled one of those lengths of hemp, it's a bit hard to appreciate the difficulty of roping a steer in rapid time from a running horse.

From this point, we move into the games and competitions likely to be found in almost any show featuring Western riding. Various breed and show associations provide rules for the events, and the skills required of both horse and rider can be quite dramatic.

Barrel racing is a good example, as the space required is not great (a total length of about seventy-five yards and a width of about thirty-five, with some runover left for safety). The American Quarter Horse Association specifies a cloverleaf pattern, with twenty-five yards from the starting line to the first barrel, thirty-five yards to the second barrel, and forty yards to the third. The first barrel is rounded clockwise, the second is rounded counterclockwise, and the third also counterclockwise with a straight dash to the start-finish line. The pattern can be reversed. Runover space should be no less than six yards at any barrel, with a twenty-yard runover at the start-finish line. (The horse will be flying along about then, and space is needed to stop safely.)

Barrel-racing champions almost never look for very young horses, with age preferences depending on the person, ranging from possibly eight on up past twelve years old. These horses are seasoned and settled, or should be, and can be easily taught the necessary patterns. Teaching the horse starts at a walk and proceeds at a trot, until both horse and rider are accustomed to each other and the patterns, at which time the horseman (in this case women are usually most successful because of their lighter weight) starts working for speed, aiming the horse about three feet to one side of the barrel so that it can roll back around the barrel without hitting it, yet doesn't need to make a huge, time-consuming circle.

Whips and spurs are used, but the best barrel racers save such urging for the last possible moment. A whipping, screaming, spurring rider may look fast, but most often the calm, controlled rider is the first one around and across the finish line.

Barrel racing is a sport that can sour a horse if too much practice is done once the patterns are learned. Generally, good conditioning methods should be used, but the patterns shouldn't be run more than once every week or two in practice.

Again, the good horseman will work with the horse, making sure the animal is in the correct lead (this is a part of learning the patterns; the leads, important to many kinds of Western riding, will be covered later), and that the rider is as still in the saddle as possible, not doing too much to counterbalance the horse's leaning in the turns. Even twisting off to one side on the ride for the finish, in preparation for using the whip, can

Fig. 8. Barrel racing takes nerve and skill on the part of both horse and rider. Credit: Harold Compton & AQHA.

cost time in a barrel race. Generally, a smooth ride will reward you with the best time, as will interfering as little as possible with the stride and concentration of the horse.

Pole bending is another timed event, this time with seven-foot-long poles, six of them, set twenty feet apart, in a straight line. The first pole is twenty feet from the start-finish line. The horse and rider face the poles at the start, and, on signal, race to the last pole, turn to the left and wind between the poles, turning at the first pole and rerunning the course. At the

Fig. 9. Pole bending is another excellent Western-style event requiring a great deal of skill. Credit: Harold Compton & AQHA.

number-six pole, they turn and head for home. In some competitions, seconds are added to the time if a pole is knocked down, while in others no penalties are assessed as long as all poles are rounded. In others, the rider has to dismount and reset the poles.

Like barrel racing, pole bending is nearly as exciting for the spectator as it is for the rider. The horses will have a lot in common with good barrel-racing horses, and, in fact, a few riders will use the same horse in both events.

Pole bending is, to my thinking, a good event for a moderately skilled rider who wishes to start timed-event competition. The danger from falling on a properly constructed pole—bases should be covered with rubber along their edges—is less than from hitting or falling on a barrel. Of course, as in any speed event, it's far better to start slow and progress in easy stages, accustoming both horse and rider to each other, and the event, over a period of time.

Flag racing can be as complex or as easy as the organizers wish. There may be different classes, too. Essentially, the simplest form requires a 100-foot space from the start-finish line, with a barrel set at the end. A flag is stuck in the barrel, and the rider simply heads for the barrel as fast as possible, does a rollback around it picking up the flag, and then returns to the finish line.

More complex forms use two flags placed at the ends of a U, with a barrel at the bottom of the U. The rider *starts* with a flag, changes flags at the bucket, races around the barrel, and changes flags once more at the final bucket before heading for the finish line. A horse with a smooth and balanced ride is essential here, but one ingredient is added, for to change flags in the buckets, you must stop and stand and then accelerate to the next station.

Keyhole racing is an event that can drive competitors insane—it looks extremely simple, but requires exquisite control of the horse. A limed circle twenty feet in diameter is used, with a four-foot-wide lane leading into the circle (in my area, the lane is only run for the six feet or so just before the horse and rider enter the circle, or keyhole, while in other areas it is marked for the entire distance—usually forty feet—from the start-finish line).

The horse must stay in the lane, enter the keyhole, stop, turn and return to the start-finish line as quickly as possible. If, at any point, the horse steps on the circle or lane it is disqualified. Keyhole racing requires at least three observers, or judges, to make sure whether or not the horse has stepped on or over the lines.

The stop and turn back used here are actually known as a rollback and to keep all that action inside a small lane and circle at a furious pace requires supreme control and a really fine horse.

Reining contests require an advanced horse and an advanced rider. They are not for beginners, though any danger is minimal. What takes reining out of the beginner's class is the requirement that a horse make a controlled sliding stop, rollback, pivot, and back up. Lead changes are also required, and they must be done correctly, something the beginning rider usually has difficulty with. Horses cannot be allowed to memorize patterns, for there are four basic patterns in the rule book (American Quarter Horse Association) and others can be added by the judges as long as the competitors are notified a specified time before the event takes place. The rider must memorize the pattern, though. A typical reining horse contest might use the following standard pattern: a full speed run, at least twenty feet from any railing, with a sliding stop at the end, after which the horse is backed up. The rider is then allowed about ten seconds to settle the horse down. The team then rides a small figure eight at a slow canter, with correct leads and lead changes. The large figure eight is ridden at a faster pace, again with correct lead changes. Next comes a left rollback, then a right rollback, another stop, either a right or left pivot, another pivot, in the opposite direction from the first. The horse is then ridden to the judge and stopped. That's pattern number one, and if you can do all that faultlessly, then you have a chance at winning. If not, forget it.

Basically a good horse can easily, with proper training, do all of that, and you should practice the patterns in and out of sequence (more out of sequence than in: you have to be able to memorize a particular pattern quickly, but it is by far better if the horse is kept to knowing just the maneuvers needed without settling on a single pattern, as the horse could refuse to ride to any other, or get confused when the patterns are changed, thus costing you a place).

Trail-horse competitions present the arena competitor with conditions simulating a trail ride of varying difficulty. It is the rider's and the horse's handling of tight places and snags that determines the winner. Various contests will include different specific individual events so that the alert rider and horse has the best chance of winning. In all classes, we can hope the organizers can keep in mind that while a trail horse should be safe and a pleasure to ride, the old plug who just doodles along shouldn't really have a chance to do well. That horse may be safe to ride, and even a pleasure to some, but it isn't what real trail riding is all about. A trail horse should move well at the walk, trot, and the lope, while being alert enough to handle most normal trail-riding difficulties.

Fig. 10. Trail-riding events approximate trail conditions when properly set up, including having horse and rider pick their way over small, closely spaced obstacles, as here. Credit: Jerry Matacale & AQHA.

Such difficulties could start with simply leading a pack horse, and continue with a rope drag of a log (carrying double might be added). In most classes, a downed timber obstacle will be set up, with the horse that carefully, but quickly, picks its way over doing the best. Gate opening could be another test, and usually is. For this, you should be able to easily position your horse so you can lean over, open the gate latch and swing the gate, ride through and then close the gate. All without dismounting. Moving through narrow lanes, often outlined with timber in an L shape, can also be added and is frequently set up so the horse will have to back over a portion of the course. In some cases, this requirement for backing will make an individual test, and the horse will have to back along the outline lane, making the turn at the corner of the L.

Other trail-riding tests are possible, including mounting and dismounting on both sides. In general, we emphasize mounting a horse from the left, or near, side in almost all types of riding, but sometimes mounting from the right, or off, side is essential. The horse must stand for this, because on a real trail the correct mounting position could place you over a drop of many feet.

Barriers made of live animals may be used. Some organizations may go so far as to rent large animals (such as mountain lions), which are then placed as trail barriers. The horse is required to ride near these animals, being alert to their presence, but without spooking.

Other combinations are possible. Trail-riding classes are among the most varied at Western shows, for trail-riding conditions can vary widely. While we don't seem to have any mountain lions left in Virginia's Blue Ridge Mountains, there are bears, and so many deer in my area that it's a hunter's paradise. The bears aren't numerous, but they are there. Having a horse that can handle such situations is a good start for a pleasant ride, for sooner or later you'll come on a deer, which will spook away, and might well spook your horse. We also have a great many smaller animals such as raccoon, fox, and so on, and these could prove a problem to a poorly trained trail horse. Trail-horse competitions should be designed to test your horse's

Fig. 11. Western pleasure classes are a fine starting point for the novice competitor, but rapidly get more difficult as you progress. Credit: Harold Compton & AQHA.

response to almost any easily imaginable situation. Good ones are.

Western pleasure horse and Western equitation classes differ markedly, though many people tend to confuse them. In fact, more than a few judges seem to confuse the two.

Western pleasure horse classes are classes in which the horse is judged, and, basically, the horse is judged on the amount of pleasure it would be to ride. No matter how clumsy the rider is, the horse is not downgraded if its reactions are correct.

Western equitation or **horsemanship** classes are a different story, for the rider is primarily the one judged in these, with the judge asking for different maneuvers to determine just how well the rider controls his horse. This class judges every aspect of riding, from the proper fit of the saddle to the rider to the correct way of holding the reins.

Obviously, in both instances there is an inner relationship, the story of all horsemanship. A poor rider has less chance of controlling even a top pleasure horse properly than does a good rider, while a poor horse is not going to make the best rider look as good as is possible. But we must remember the emphasis in each class. If the world's worst rider has a Western pleasure horse that is perfect, and behaves perfectly, then that horse should place rather high, though it would be unlikely to win.

The foregoing covers a few of the different types of competitive events, both simple show and timed, that a Western horseman might find of interest. There are others, quite a few others, with the actual events varying as to the organization and the area of the country in which a show is held. Still, probably something under 10 percent of all riders participate in shows. What happens to the rest of us? The answers vary, but some of the classes to be found in shows will provide a start at finding out.

Western trail-horse classes are more and more popular, and the simple reason for that is the increased number of riders actually taking to the trails.

There is little that can compare with saddling up and heading out for a few hours, or many hours, on trails in areas of the United States and Canada. Trails include the verge of a country lane, a dirt road winding through some low hills in the East, the broken mountain country of Arizona, or the mountains of California. You name it, and you'll find a horse and rider there. After all, if New York City can have mounted police, then there is space to ride almost everywhere. In fact, New York City provides numerous trails for other riders as well.

Suburban horses are becoming more popular, and their growth in numbers there may be the largest reason for the great increase in the number of horses in the United States over the past decade or so. Most such horses get little riding time, and often, the only way to get to any kind of long-distance trail is to take the horse there by trailer. Horse-trailer companies are doing quite well.

Even where I live, in a rural area, it sometimes pays to trailer a horse a number of miles to find trails one hasn't seen too often. In other areas, it's possible to ride most of the day without crossing your own tracks—or those of others.

The psychological reasoning behind all this equine/human activity may be simple or complex. Personally, I feel a lot of it is simply because we've come so far from what we were, and there is a strong desire to return to some sort of roots, to put down tendrils into the more natural lives we managed to leave behind decades ago. In addition, horses provide a tension release of the most positive kind. A fast canter, or even a gallop when conditions are right, can blow away a lot of mental ashes that accumulate during a nine-to-five day when the boss growls, his secretary snaps, and the bill collectors howl. A long walk on horseback can do much the same, calming the nerves while giving a gentle and beneficial massage to muscles that are otherwise seldom used.

In part, the increasing popularity of Western riding could also be a desire to return to the simplicity, or seeming simplicity, of the days of open range. Another way of playing cowboys and Indians, possibly.

As with many recreational activities, analysis of the reasons is not essential, and may in fact be self-defeating. If you enjoy something and it harms no one else, it can seldom do more than provide a benefit. Horseback riding certainly falls into the scheme, as the exercise is beneficial, and the relationship to an animal that has been for thousands of years a companion and servant of mankind and the relationship with like-minded people (or the chance for simple solitude) should be of help to many of us. It is to me.

Expense, though, becomes a consideration. Keeping a horse today isn't cheap. Back in my grandfather's day, almost everyone rode, and most people living outside of cities kept horses (and it wasn't all that long ago). Hay and grains were cheap, but then so was almost everything else. Still, with management, and luck, the cost of owning a horse can probably be kept to as little as $500 a year today, though some forms of competition and types of riding immediately jack this into the $1,000 range. A recent estimate of the cost of keeping a horse today claimed that the cost hit $1,500 per year in many cases. That survey was taken by a financial paper, though, and one that probably got most of its information from city dwellers and owners of the more expensive breeds who would tend to invest a great deal of money in stable fees (if you live in a city, you seldom have the pasture needed to hold even one horse, so a stable is essential, while a move to suburbia at least saves the stable fee, though you'll probably have to buy grain or hay or both year round).

The cost is going to vary, for a heavy vet's bill can run a yearly total out of sight. And your desires may not be the same as mine. You may really want one of those $2,000 show saddles, instead of my $400 roughout roper.

Whatever, and we'll go into more detail on costs later on, the cost should be a carefully figured item, for an unaffordable horse is likely to be a mistreated horse. If you can't pay for a vet when the horse is ill, things become complex. If you can't afford feed in winter, then trouble will arise.

You'll need, as we all do, an examination of your resources before getting into horses by owning your own. One thing should be kept in mind, though it is more a maxim for horse breeders than for backyard owners: it costs no more to feed a top-quality horse than to feed a sack-of-bones hayburner that can't do what you want it to.

2. HORSES FOR WESTERN RIDING

In a sense, almost any horse can be used to ride in the Western manner. At one time or another, I would even bet on someone having used a Belgian draft horse, while it's not all that unusual to see Thoroughbreds, Saddlebreds, and so on under a Western saddle and heading into the sunset.

Even so, and particularly for competitive events, some breeds have a definite running start over others—and maintain the advantage on through any kind of use a Western horseman may want. That isn't to say that one particular breed is necessarily better than another overall. It's more accurate to state that for the particular purposes in mind, a horse developed for those purposes will do a better job than one developed for some other purpose.

That still leaves an enormous choice of breeds, for a quick check through the latest list of light-horse breeds in the all-breed issue of *Western Horseman* magazine shows about forty-two breed associations and registries that cover the various light-horse breeds. Some of these are obvious duplicates, with a registry doing one job and the association doing another (in the case of Arabian horses), and others being more or less competing registries or associations (as is the case with the two Quarter Horse associations). In other cases, I'm not even certain any horseman will consider the horses registered as true breeds (in one case, Rangerbreds, the association makes no

such claim, and allows a wide range of horses to be registered).
The horse industry is extremely fragmented, and the prolifera-
tion of breed associations indicates this quite well.

Generally, a true breed is considered to be one in which one
or several foundation sires have provided what is known as
prepotency, a strong tendency for their get to retain desirable
characteristics through many generations. Probably the supreme example of this is the Morgan horse. Justin Morgan, of
West Springfield, Massachusetts, is known today only because
of a single stud he owned, also called Justin Morgan. This is the
only horse who has given his name to a recognized breed, and
his record for prepotency is unmatched. The breed exists today
in much the same form as the original Justin Morgan did in the
eighteenth century. Generally, today's Morgan is a small breed,
standing fourteen to fifteen hands, and seldom weighing more
than a thousand pounds, more often 800 to 900.

One strain of Morgans has been developed as a Western-
style horse, or cow pony, and until the University of Vermont
began working with the breed there were more Morgans in the
West than in the East where they originated. Even with today's
variation in appearance, Morgans retain much of the delicate
head style, tapering neck, short legs, short back, and other
features of Justin Morgan.

To go further into prepotency brings one to the Arabian
horse. This superb breed is the foundation breed for almost all
other light breeds—a widely divergent group that includes
Thoroughbreds and Quarter Horses, as two extreme examples.
Just as no one knows Justin Morgan's exact lineage, no one
knows the exact time and place that the Arabian horse came
into being. He is presumed to have cropped up first in India,
and selective breeding practices are said to have taken place
with Arabians as far back as the time of Mohammed (*ca.* A.D.
600), a goodly number of years in horse generations. Mythol-
ogy credits the birth of the Arabian horse to the West Wind,
and I find this an attractive fantasy.

Watching an Arabian, with its small head, curved and
pointed ears, small muzzle, and well-set eyes, is an unrivaled
pleasure. This free-galloping horse, with its flaring nostrils,

beautiful stride, and flowing mane and tail can be described only in superlatives, and is best experienced rather than described. Riding this most intelligent of all breeds is extraordinary, for though hot-blooded, they are gentle and willing, strong and fast.

If this sounds as if I love Arabians above all other breeds, so be it. This is a horse that can, and has, done everything and will do more. And it does it all with panache, a totality of style that I find lacking in many other breeds. None of this is meant to take away from other breeds, for at some jobs they can surpass Arabians (a Quarter Horse of the old style, with its catty build, will stop faster, turn more quickly, and accelerate over short distances more rapidly, while Thoroughbreds will flat hammer almost any Arabian into a race track of most any kind if the length reaches a mile, or if there are high jumps to be taken). Still, as an all-around horse, the Arabian can't be beat. It can work cattle, provide pleasure rides, win shows of any kind. In fact, I'm somewhat of the opinion that the only reason more Arabians aren't on the Western show circuit (in all- or general-breed shows) is simply because they tend to be quite expensive in relation to the stock horse breeds, and very high in relation to the basic grade horse (unregistered). I have a friend who raises Arabians and I still cannot afford one, though I have hopes for the future.

As an example of probable prices, and a lead into another fine breed, we can examine the prices for champion bloodline Appaloosas: I note that not far from here, a nine-year-old mare is going for $1,150. That's an Ap, with champion Quarter Horse blood also. Of one thing I'm sure, though, and that is that this is no finished horse. She's a broodmare, probably gentle and easily ridden. Prices for such champion Appaloosas can range up to about $2,500, but most are closer to $1,000, and may be down around $500 in some cases. Late last year I had to turn down a chance to buy a superb Ap for $800 simply because I lacked the space and time to care for her. I would doubt, today, that you could touch a good Arabian filly or mare for under $2,500, with prices scooting as high as $10,000 and more.

For the average person even the champion bloodlines of some less expensive breeds are out of sight. What should be emphasized here, and strongly, is that *good* bloodlines, in a horse with good conformation and manners, or even unknown bloodlines, can be just as satisfactory as the fanciest pedigree in the world. Many people, most people, are just as satisfied and just as well off with a grade horse as with the top cutting horse or the top reining horse in any breed.

The reason is a simple one. Such top horses require constant "tuning up" if they're to stay on top, and most of us simply haven't got the time, or experience, to allow for that sort of work. Too, if someone is about to get his or her first horse, there is little or no sense in getting a very expensive, finished horse, for much riding experience is needed before you'll begin to be able to take advantage of those skills, and, as time passes and your superbly trained horse doesn't get to use its skills, it will become untrained, or detrained. In other words, at the outset it doesn't pay to overhorse yourself.

Appaloosas are a colorful breed of horses, both in appearance and historically. The Appaloosa Horse Club was founded in 1938 and is the official breed registry. The first stud book came out in 1947 and has had to be supplemented some twenty times since. It is one of the fastest-growing breeds around for a variety of reasons. First, the horses are still reasonable in price, while gaining in value as breed acceptance increases. Second, the Appaloosa is an extremely attractive and desirable horse from just about any standpoint.

Originally known as the Nez Perce war-horse, Appaloosas are noted for stamina, courage, and quiet dispositions. In fact, it is said that children of the Nez Percé used to be able to mount these horses by climbing their tails, an example of an extremely quiet disposition in any tailed animal! After Chief Joseph's defeat and capture in 1877, the breed was dispersed and almost disappeared. Since 1938, breed numbers have increased dramatically, with over a quarter of a million horses registered since then. Thus Aps form the third-largest breed in the U.S. today (Quarter Horses lead with well over a million horses registered since the breed began, and Thoroughbreds come second with nearly three-quarters of a million registered and about 38,000 added each year; from there, the numbers decrease with one or two registries having no more than seventy-five horses).

Of one thing you can be sure. If you see an Appaloosa, you'll know just what breed it is, for there is just no way to mistake the distinctive characteristics of appearance of this breed. Generally, a horse with an eye encircled by white is considered undesirable and is almost certain to have a poor disposition, yet in Appaloosas this white circling is a breed characteristic (as it is in the Paint and Pinto). The skin of an Ap is mottled, irregularly spotted in black and white, most easily noticed around the nostrils. Hooves have distinctive vertical black and white striping. While coat patterns vary widely, the most usual patterns show a white blanket over the hips, with dark spots on this blanket. Some Appaloosas may be leopard spotted all over the body. No two are marked alike, and the patterns tend to change from year to year.

Buckskin horses also originated in the United States and are registered with the American Buckskin Registry Association or the International Buckskin Horse Association. Generally a Quarter Horse type, the Buckskin will be a claybank dun, a grulla (a mouse dun), or buckskin, sometimes with a dorsal stripe (often called a zebra dun).

Paint and Pinto horses also have distinctive markings, setting them well apart from other breeds. Two distinct patterns are recognized for the markings. Overo patterned horses have white markings extending upward from the belly. Tobiano horses have their primary white marking extending downward from their backs. Both may have other white markings.

Palominos are golden in color, with light-colored manes and tails that cannot have more than 15 percent chestnut hairs if the horse is to be registered. My wife, Caroline, informs me that Palominos cannot be considered a true breed, as the color will not breed true between two of them. This may bring argument, but as she's the geneticist in the family I have no choice but to accede.

Quarter Horses are the horses of the American cowboys in many peoples' minds, and with justification. The American Quarter Horse racing offering the highest prizes in racing—the registered over 1¼ million horses, with 1978 registrations expected, for the first time, to exceed 100,000. Some 2,100 breed shows are held each year, and there is even an American Junior Quarter Horse Association with more than 6,000 members.

There are, today, two types of Quarter Horses. One is the short-coupled, strong-legged descendant of the originals, while the other is a longer-legged, longer-bodied racing model. With Quarter Horse racing offering the highet prizes in racing—the 1977 All American Futurity paid the winner $437,500—we can expect more development along Thoroughbred lines, especially as total prize money at a 1979 Los Alamitos race is expected to reach $750,000. These are the runners, but the show horses in other forms of competition don't come away broke, either. The 1978 World Championship Quarter Horse show offered prize money totalling $175,000, with Skoal/Copenhagen adding another $5,000 for the most versatile horse.

Quarter Horse prices have risen in recent years, as have the prices of almost all good horses, but even with the supremely expensive show mounts, you can usually find a Quarter Horse to fit just about any budget that can really afford a horse. This horse, in its original form, has a heavily muscled body with a powerful bone structure, small ears, and often heavily muscled jaws and cheeks. Their name derives from their abilities in short dashes, and this is combined with nicely spread hooves and strong legs to allow them to be less fragile under range-style riding than are some other breeds.

For anyone interested in Western riding, the Quarter Horse is close to an ideal choice, with price reasonable and abilities high.

Additionally, the Quarter Horse is cold-blooded, which means it will be easier to handle and somewhat more gentle than Thoroughbreds or Arabians. And the classic Quarter Horse tends to be what is known as an easy keeper. That is, if the horse's health is good, you will find it needs less feed to stay fit than will a comparable horse of some other breeds (for example, a Thoroughbred usually burns up more nervous energy and will require more feed per pound of horse than will your Quarter Horse).

Quarter Horse color can vary all over the lot, though excessive white markings in certain areas and Appaloosa markings will disqualify a horse from the breed. Most common colors are chestnut, bay, and dun, but you'll also see black, palomino, roan, brown, and coppery-colored Quarter Horses.

Rangerbreds, of which there are only a few hundred in the country, are very similar in marking and type to the Appaloosa, but color is not a breed requirement.

Spanish-Barbs are small horses, to the point where other breed associations would consider them ponies (height standards are 13-3 to 14-1). Muscling isn't heavy, but the body is deep. There are, possibly, fifty or sixty of these small, durable horses in the U.S. today. The most common colors are dun, grulla, and sorrel.

The Mustang is a descendant of the feral horse of the Plains, or is said to be. These are, again, small horses, with heights ranging from 13 to about 14½ hands. Color is not a requirement for registry, so they can be found in just about any color you will ever see on an equine. There are about 500 of these sturdy horses registered today.

Thoroughbreds are considered the aristocrats of the equine world, and, as such, are not often considered for Western riding and pleasure use. Publicized prices are enough to scare most people away, with some sales drawing averages of more than $125,000 for yearlings in 1978.

Those prices, though, are for horses headed for racetracks or headed for breeding farms where racetrack prospects are the special aims of the owners. Not every Thoroughbred is such a prospect, and not every owner wishes them to be. Those are the people you need to search out if you wish to use one of these horses for Western riding. Still, in relation to stock and grade horses, the prices will be high, probably starting at over $2,500.

Riding the average Thoroughbred around stock horses can be an experience, for the average stock horse is probably about fifteen hands, give or take a bit, and the average Thoroughbred tends to run up near sixteen hands. In some cases, as my recent transfer from a friend's 14-1 Ap mare to a sixteen-hand Thoroughbred gelding, the difference seems really extreme!

That's only seven inches (a hand is four inches, supposedly the span of the average person's hand), but you tend to feel as if a stepladder would be handy in mounting when you've gotten used to smaller horses.

Thoroughbred acceleration tends to be slower than the stock horse's, but the top speed is greater and can be held over a somewhat longer period of time if the terrain permits (and your nerve holds out). They are generally more spirited and can thus be harder to handle for inexperienced riders, though many are used as children's mounts. Again breed characteristics are one thing, individual animals are another. A friend's Quarter Horse is often harder to handle than are his Thoroughbreds.

Other breeds are suitable for Western riding, but because of numbers and general training are seldom used. While I've never ridden one, a friend keeps a Tennessee Walking Horse on which he tosses a Western saddle when he wishes to go any distance. That running walk, a breed characteristic, is a great comfort when you wish to put thirty miles or more behind you in a day.

A rather recent breed—since 1948—the Missouri Fox Trotting horse has an odd, broken, but comfortable gait that makes it good for long-distance riding. Basically the Missouri Fox Trotter walks with its front feet and trots with its hind feet, with a rather low action and a nodding head. The gait is said to be extremely comfortable.

The Racking Horse came into being as a breed about a decade ago. It is extremely popular in my area of the country and has a running walk similar to, but not quite the same, as the Tennessee Walker. The gait is a four-beat action, not quite a trot or a pace; the rider seems almost to be suspended on air and there is little body jarring.

The American Saddle Horse began being registered in 1891, and is a showy breed, with a long, finely muscled neck, a high-stepping action, and a high-set tail. The gait used to cover ground is very smooth, though with the high lift to the hooves it would appear that isn't possible.

The Paso Fino horse is another exceptionally smooth-gaited breed, with a broken, four-beat gait. This particular broken gait, though, is a lateral one, with the legs on the same side moving together, and the hind hoof striking the ground a fraction of a second before the front hoof does.

On top of all these breeds, there are various ponies and other breeds, usually based on half one kind of ancestry and half another (American Morab is half Morgan and part Arabian, for example). A few registries are started simply because someone has a horse he wishes to register and no other group will accept it. We can assume that, if these registries are run properly and the breed has some outstanding characteristic at the outset, a few will last and provide us with other, valuable breeds of horses in the future.

One other horse breed needs to be covered before going on to conformation and other characteristics to look for when buying a horse—the grade horse. Actually, the grade horse is not a breed. It is simply an unregistered horse, of whatever breeding happened to come along. In other words, a plain, old-fashioned horse of the working kind. In numbers, the grade horse is the most prevalent, and often in working capabilities and other characteristics as good, or better than, registered horses of many kinds. A grade horse can even be a pureblood, though one without papers. Registries will often deny papers to horses showing excessive markings of one type or another, which adds another inexpensive, but fine, horse to the legions already available. Papers don't make a horse. They never have and they never will. Too many horse owners seem to forget that today's breeds came from unregistered stock—no one knows the true breeding of Justin Morgan, just as no one knows the exact breeding of the Godolphin Barb, one of the foundation sires of the modern Thoroughbred.

Unless you plan to breed horses, then, papers are of less importance than the overall quality of the horse you're looking at. A good grade horse is a better buy, by far, than is a mediocre breed horse with a fistful of papers showing its great, great, great granddaddy was such and whatever. While correct breeding procedures certainly have more than just a tendency to keep desirable characteristics in a line, you can do as well, or better if you are a beginner, by selecting a grade horse.

Many of the top reining and cutting horses, and roping horses and . . . simply many horses are grade horses. After all, with possibly as many as 10 million horses in this country and not more than 2.5 million registered horses, someone somewhere has to be pleased with the grade horse.

SELECTING YOUR HORSE

We've gone over a lot of information on breeds and there is a lot more of that available, directly from the breed associations (you'll find an up-to-date list at the end of this chapter, including pony associations). But selecting a breed or deciding on a grade horse is far from all there is to know about selecting the correct horse for your needs. As a matter of fact, deciding on the breed and price range are among the first, and easiest, decisions, though you may find that to get what you want your price range needs to be a bit higher or somewhat more flexible than you anticipate.

We're gearing this section to the prospective horse owner, but those of you who don't wish to own your own for whatever reasons shouldn't totally avoid it. A lot of the information on conformation and other characteristics can make your selection of steeds at the local riding stable a simpler chore, and can result in more satisfying rides.

The complexities of horse selection decrease as you gain experience, or at least seem to, as you learn more and become more confident of your own decisions. The horse you buy as a beginner will probably not do at all in a very short time, but selecting an expert's horse at the outset is never a good idea. First, all that expensive training must be paid for and won't get used, eventually getting lost in the process of *your* learning. Second, you'll be over your head. The horse will react to cues you don't even know you're giving it, which is often a very good way of finding yourself seated on the ground instead of in the saddle. I can remember a time, some twenty years ago, when I had very little saddle time in (and hadn't even been on a horse for about six or seven years, as a matter of fact). Some service friends decided a ride would be a good idea and convinced me to come along. They also decided that a little amusement was in order.

My horse was a reasonable-looking animal, a bay, with a white snip. All saddled and waiting next to the fence, as my friends swung up. So I stuck a toe in the stirrup and swung aboard myself. My right foot never hit the stirrup. That horse had an action I can only describe as an elevator gone mad, and took only about four good crow hops and one-half a sunfish to deposit me over that barbed-wire fence. Which proved a good time to be thankful for the durability of denim in heavy weights and a body conditioned by a couple of years in the Marines.

I discovered, when two friends rolled out of their saddles holding their sides and screaming with laughter, that my horse was one of the top rodeo-bucking horses in the area. More horse than I could handle then (and probably now). Part of the point is simply that my friends could have saved themselves a lot of trouble in trailering a good bucking horse fifteen miles to the stable. Simply placing me on a good roping horse would likely have had the same effect should I have managed to cue it incorrectly.

So start by considering your own level of skill. For beginners, an older horse, and certainly never one under eight years old, with preference given to ten or twelve, is sure to be more settled and easier to ride. Don't kid yourself that an older horse is going to be too slow at the outset, either, for eight to twelve is not old in horse lifetimes—rather, it is maturity and the prime of life all combined. Right now, I spend a lot of time on a friend's fourteen-year-old buckskin (a grade horse by the way). Ol' Boy tends to laziness, but a good cueing will set him to moving about as fast as I care to go most days, and he's surefooted, easy to catch, easy to saddle, and about as well mannered as a horse can be. He was well trained at some time in the past, though neither his owner nor I have any idea where or by whom.

Call yourself a first-level rider. You've been in the saddle a few times, but have no confidence in your ability to maintain your balance at much more than a fast walk, and still tend to let your heels rise, with an occasional tug at the reins for security's sake (knock that off immediately as it's the worst thing you can do).

At this stage, a grade horse, or one of the cold-blooded breeds, will be your best choice. Cold-blooded breeds are the stock-horse types such as the Quarter Horse and Appaloosa (Arabians and Thoroughbreds are considered hot-blooded). Again, you have to make sure of the individual horse's temperament, and a lot of half-bred animals make great beginners' horses, as can some Arabians.

Generally, look for a gelding, as their temperaments tend to be the easiest going of all horses. Oddly enough, though, you do not want a beginning horse that will refuse to move out on cue (Ol' Boy wouldn't be ideal for the beginning rider, as it would require too much effort to get him moving well most of the time).

Because the beginning rider is liable to be hard on the horse's mouth, a highly trained animal is unsuitable, no matter the age. Most highly trained horses are used to being ridden by experts (in many cases, an expert rider with a well-trained mount will not allow anyone else to ride that animal, at least until such time as that rider is certain the candidate for riding has a good pair of hands).

Shifting weight unnecessarily to maintain balance, grabbing at the saddle horn, using the legs to cling to the horse, and sawing at the reins are all things done by just about every unskilled rider, and all of these things can end up with a horse used to an expert rider simply putting the beginner in the dirt.

At the same time, the beginners' mount should have good, solid, basic training in neck reining, stopping, backing, and going forward, as well as changing gaits on cue.

In other words, the beginners' horse is going to be hard to locate, and you may have to start with more of a plug than you really desire. You need a horse that will go, and go easily and quietly, but one that will not insist that you be easy and quiet on its back. At this stage, you must make unreasonable demands on the horse and can't afford any that the horse may make on you, for a good buck or two will probably see you on the ground.

Your size should have some relation to the size of the horse, if for no other reason than too-short legs on a tall horse have a hard time reaching down to the area where cues are given the animal. Too, feeling you need to find a rock or box to mount and dismount gets old quickly. I've mentioned the feeling that I needed a stepladder to mount some Thoroughbreds, even those no taller than sixteen hands, and that is a slight exaggeration, as my legs are fairly long, but I still, at 6'2", feel more comfortable on a fifteen-hand horse. And I don't feel at all uneasy on a horse as small as fourteen hands, as long as it is short-coupled and heavily muscled enough to bear my weight (not all tall horses are as strong, inch for inch and pound for pound, as shorter horses).

Possibly my ego might get a boost from being stuck up on a horse seventeen hands tall but I really doubt it. More likely I'd just feel as if I were going to topple over. I don't ride to boost my ego, but for the enjoyment I receive in other ways, so I tend to stick with smaller horses whenever I can.

Shorter riders wanting an ego boost can go ahead and ride what they wish, as can anyone, but that ego elevation is going to descend suddenly the day they find themselves with a toe in one stirrup and a restless, capering horse making them jump all over the lot before they can mount.

Your first horse should, as I've said, be a gelding; usually, though, there's no real reason for not selecting a mare if she's well settled. Young mares may tend to be fractious in some company, though, and may be a little harder to control than a gelding. In no case should a novice rider ever so much as consider getting a stallion. While a well-trained stallion should be no big problem for the experienced rider, such an animal will just about always be more than the inexperienced person can control.

When looking your prospective first horse over, check its manners while being groomed, led, and generally handled. He should give his feet willingly for a check of the hooves and for hoof cleaning (a small chore of great importance to the health of the horse, and, unfortunately, one that too many riders don't bother with as often as necessary—a minimum of a check before the ride and after the ride, with cleaning as needed).

The first horse for the beginning rider should also have

comfortable gaits. A walk is generally no trouble, but the trot
and canter may be. If at all possible, you should ride the horse
for a few minutes yourself. If your skills aren't advanced
enough to canter the animal, you'll be wise to bring along a
friend who has more skill. If the animal is barn sour—has a
tendency to want to stay in the barn area, or to return to it at an
uncontrollable run—or heads for fences, or corners, to try to
rub off its rider, now's the time to find out. Look for smoothness in the trot and canter; some horses have naturally rough
and choppy gaits and there is just about nothing to be done to
correct this tendency. Check the horse to make sure it will
stand while you mount and dismount and then remount.
There's nothing quite like having a hat blow off, getting down
to retrieve it, and having a horse that fiddlefoots all over a half
acre or more.

Stall the horse and check to see it doesn't try to crowd you
when you enter; a stall-trained horse should move its rump
over as soon as it realizes you are entering the stall, but take the
precaution with horses you don't know of not entering stalls
when the horse is standing with its rump to you. The horses
I've been working with lately tend to spoil me, as they do not
kick, but there are plenty around that have never been trained
not to kick (a short and easy process most of the time). Getting
kicked takes much of the fun out of riding and can be a cause of
tragedy.

Once all the foregoing is considered, you can start checking
the horse over for conformation, scars, and any other signs of
old injuries or illness, as well as checking the teeth for the
animal's age.

Sizing up a horse should follow a system, starting with a
check of its front, then one side, then the back, and then the
other side. Breed variations must be considered when looking
over a horse, as an Arabian will have a smaller head in propor-
tion to the rest of its body than will a Quarter Horse.

Look over the head, with good conformation showing in the
overall shape of the head and a clean appearance. The jaw
breadth should be good, and the jaw should be well muscled.
Ears should be of moderate or small size, depending on the

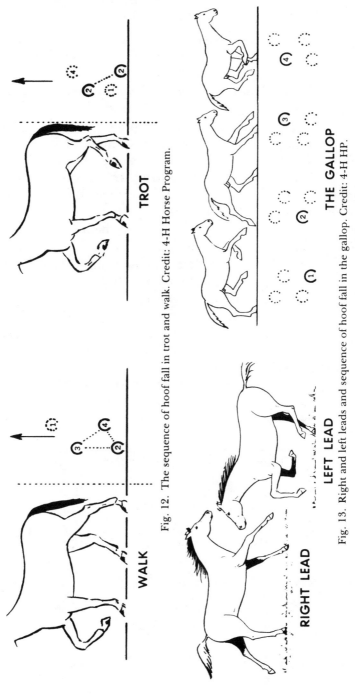

WALK

TROT

Fig. 12. The sequence of hoof fall in trot and walk. Credit: 4-H Horse Program.

RIGHT LEAD

LEFT LEAD

THE GALLOP

Fig. 13. Right and left leads and sequence of hoof fall in the gallop. Credit: 4-H HP.

breed, and should be carried alertly. An alert horse will move its ears to follow sounds. In any breed other than Appaloosas and Paints, the horse should have almost no white showing around the eyes. The neck should be muscular and proportioned to the rest of the body and the head.

Common faults of the head include undershot jaw (the lower jaw will be longer than the upper), parrot mouth (the upper jaw will be longer than the lower), blindness, moon blindness, and poll evil (the poll is the top of the head, and this condition is an inflammation usually brought on by bruising). Blindness can be determined by checking the horse's reaction as you move through its range of vision. Don't expect the horse to have the same range of vision as a human does, though. Essentially, the area of vision does *not* include the horse's mouth and it cannot see directly to its rear without turning its head.

Moon blindness is harder to check, as it may not be evident at the time of purchase. Properly named periodic opthalmia, this is a recurring condition, and may be indicated by a cloudy or inflamed eye. Some recent studies indicate that the major cause of moon blindness is the hairlike worm called Onchocerca. Generally this worm lives in the connective tissue of the neck, but migration may bring it to the eye where the

ALL THESE HORSES HAVE
UNDESIRABLE CHARACTERISTICS

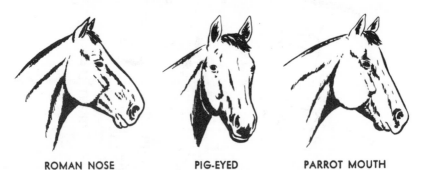

ROMAN NOSE   PIG-EYED   PARROT MOUTH

Fig. 14. Common head faults. Credit: 4-H.

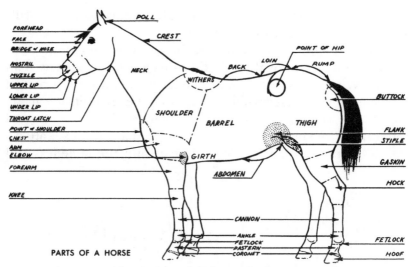

PARTS OF A HORSE

POLL, FOREHEAD, FACE, BRIDGE w NOSE, CREST, NOSTRIL, MUZZLE, UPPER LIP, LOWER LIP, UNDER LIP, THROAT LATCH, POINT w SHOULDER, CHEST, ARM, ELBOW, FOREARM, KNEE, NECK, WITHERS, SHOULDER, BARREL, GIRTH, ABDOMEN, BACK, LOIN, POINT OF HIP, RUMP, THIGH, BUTTOCK, FLANK, STIFLE, GASKIN, HOCK, CANNON, ANKLE, FETLOCK, PASTERN, CORONET, FETLOCK, HOOF

Fig. 15. Parts of the horse. Credit: 4-H.

parasite dies and causes cloudiness. Look for cloudiness in the eye; routine worming will help prevent this condition if it isn't already present.

Now your check moves to the chest area. You want to find a deep and wide chest, with the legs set straight and square. If the legs aren't set straight, the chest is narrow or the legs are crooked, and the horse has poor conformation.

Legs can and often are the sites of other problems. Check for bowed tendons, which will show as swellings of the tendons behind the cannon bones (this can occur in both front and hind legs). Sidebones are hardened, lateral cartilages directly above and to the rear quarter of the coronet. A quittor is a running sore, deep-seated and located at the coronet, while ringbone is a bony growth on the pastern bone that is seldom seen anywhere but on the front feet. A wind puff is an enlargement of the fluid sac (bursa) just above the pastern. Splints are bony growths on the cannon bone and are usually found on the insides of the front legs; large splints can cause lameness, and too often you'll see a horse that has been pin-fired to destroy the nerves in the area so the lameness will be corrected (the splints are not cured).

Buck-kneed horses have knees that bend forward, while calf-kneed horses have just the opposite.

A capped elbow is a swelling at the point of the elbow.

Of course, some of these indications are more serious than others. Wind puffs, unless extreme, are generally not a reason for rejecting a horse, while splints may be. A quittor can be cured, but ringbone can cause permanent lameness. Bowed tendons cause lameness, but the tendons may take a set after a period of time, usually at least a year, and the lameness will

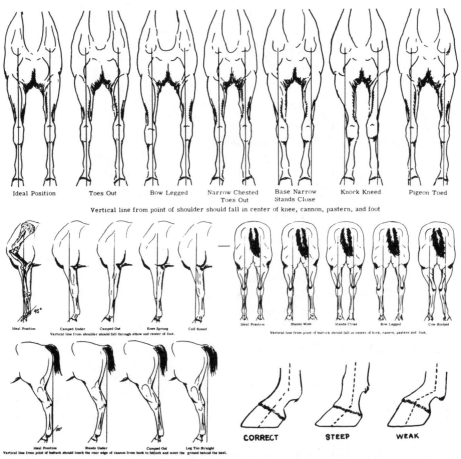

Fig. 16. Leg, chest, and rear quarter sets, both desirable and undesirable. Credit: 4-H.

PARTS OF THE PASTERN AND FOOT

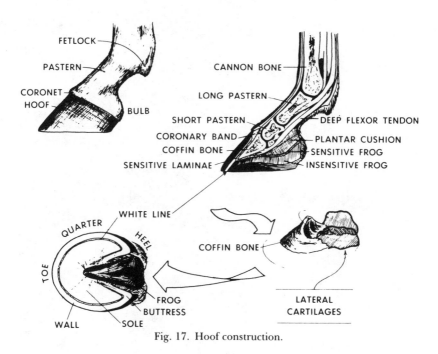

Fig. 17. Hoof construction.

FOUNDERED HOOF
Fig. 18. A foundered hoof. Credit: 4-H.

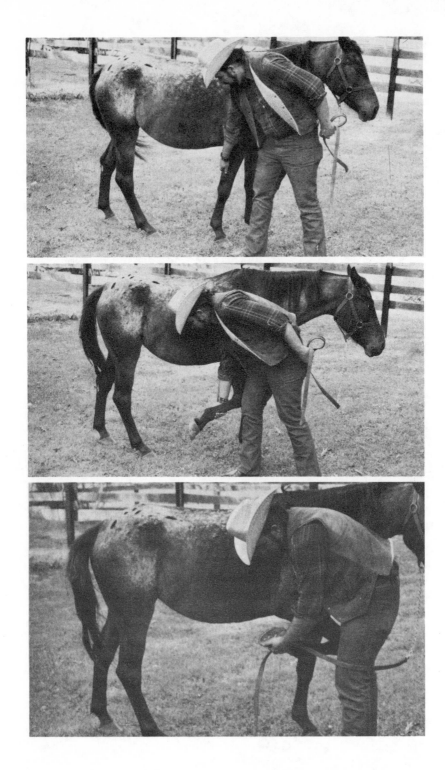

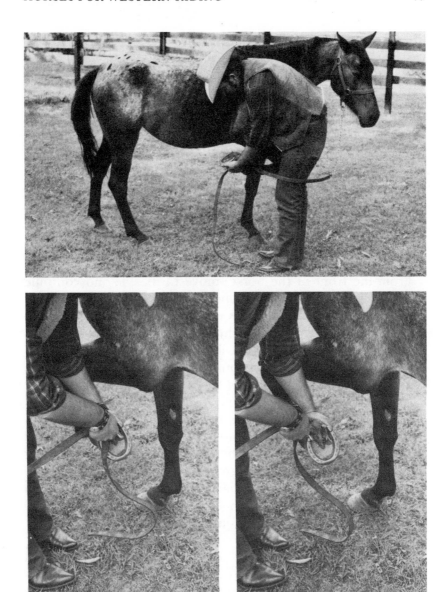

Figs. 19-24. Jim Shands raises and cleans one of Patches' front hooves, with no aid. Notice that the lead rope remains in his hand, but is *not* wrapped around the hand, even though Patches is so gentle she tends to fall asleep as her feet are cleaned.

disappear, though it will probably return if the horse is used extremely hard. The animal will, if the tendons have set, often be quite suitable for general beginners' uses. Sidebones don't generally cause lameness, and the condition is treated with special shoes and, sometimes, grooving along the sides of the hoof.

Various scars and other blemishes will usually be found on an older horse. Capped elbows are generally not found to interfere with the use of the horse, but may turn into a shoe boil after further injury. Generally, increasing the amount of bedding supplied (the injury is most often caused by the horse bringing the elbow into contact with a hard surface as it gets up) and treating the injury as an open wound will stop this problem.

From the front of the horse, move to its side and continue your check. Lift a front hoof and check for problems there. A good hoof in good condition is easily identified, for it will have no acrid odors (a sign of thrush) and no more than a few small cracks. The width of the hoof will be good, and the heels won't be pulled in or contracted. You may find bruises on the hoof, caused by using the horse over rough areas at too fast a pace. Cracks are named for the spot on the hoof in which they appear, thus you may find toe, quarter, or heel cracks. Cracks usually develop from the ground up, though it is possible, if the coronary band is injured, for them to develop from the coronet down. Cracks don't actually grow back together, so different techniques are used to immobilize the crack so that new horn growing doesn't also crack (hooves, at least the horny part, grow much like our fingernails and the cracked part can eventually be trimmed off).

Founder, or laminitis, is a common cause of lameness in horses, and will be covered in detail later because of its importance and the relative ease of its prevention. It is an inflammation of the sensitive laminae of the hoof and causes the horse extreme pain. Any horse that appears to be walking on its heels should be suspected of being foundered since most of the pain occurs in the area of the toe.

Check the area of the withers for a condition known as

Figs. 25-27. Jim raises a hind leg to check the hoof. Note that when the foot is fully raised he tips the toe up a slight bit, which makes inspection and working on the hoof easier.

fistulous withers. This is an inflammation or an infection brought on by injury or an improperly fitted harness.

Look for cocked ankles, usually at the hind legs, though sometimes in front. The fetlocks are forward, in a cocked position.

A sweeny is a depression at the shoulder brought on by

atrophied muscle tissue. Unless the condition is bad enough to cause lameness, it is not a cause for rejecting an animal. Fistulous withers may be if the inflammation is serious, for the only cure for a bad case is radical surgery.

Once you've checked the side of the horse, noting the head carriage, the activity of the ears, and the blending together of the body parts, it's getting near time to move on. First take a look at the slope of the shoulders, which should be set at a forty-five-degree angle. The topline of the horse's back should be short and strong looking, and the animal should have short coupling (the last rib should be close to the hip). The middle should be of good size and the ribs must be well sprung. From the side, the legs should be squarely set, and the pasterns will have about a forty-five-degree slope, while the horse in general must conform to its breed type.

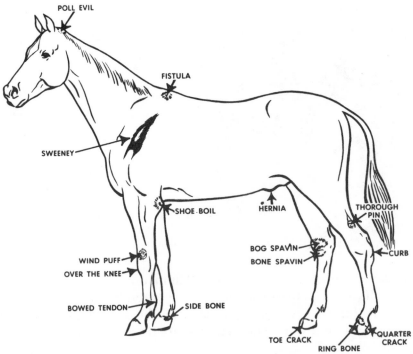

Fig. 28. Unsoundnesses and blemishes of the horse. Credit: 4-H.

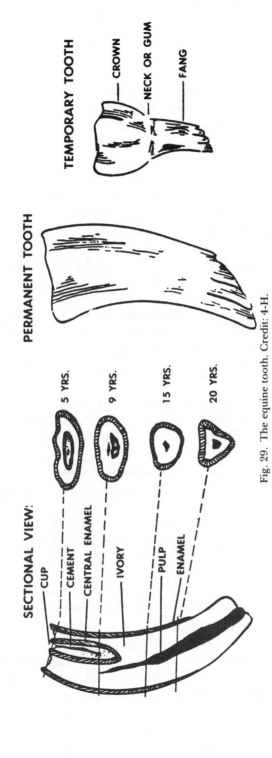

Fig. 29. The equine tooth. Credit: 4-H.

TEMPORARY TOOTH

CROWN

NECK OR GUM

FANG

PERMANENT TOOTH

SECTIONAL VIEW:

CUP

CEMENT

CENTRAL ENAMEL

IVORY

PULP

ENAMEL

5 YRS.

9 YRS.

15 YRS.

20 YRS.

When you walk to the rear of the horse check to see that it is wide and muscular over the croup and through its rear quarters, with the legs set straight and true. The tail set should conform to breed type (some are set higher than others). Long flowing tails are attractive, but go against breed type in Appaloosas, which are partly characterized by short manes and short tails.

At the rear, you can check for other blemishes: look, first, for stifles. In this case, the patella or cap of the stifle joint will have been displaced. Straight stifle joints are the cause and a recurring stifle problem may need surgery to correct it.

Checking for stringhalt requires that the horse be in motion, as it is an excessive upward flexing of the hind legs when the animal moves backward or forward. The cause isn't known, but sometimes surgery can alleviate this jerky motion.

Bone spavin is a bony enlargement on the inside of the hock at the point where the hock tapers into the cannon bone. Bone spavin seldom causes permanent lameness.

Thoroughpin is a puffing of the web of tissue of the hock, and is a blemish and not often a good reason for rejecting an animal. Bog spavin is a swelling and filling of the natural depression at the front inside of the hock, and is thought to be caused by strain. Unless pressure is extreme, this can usually be considered a blemish.

Move on to the last side of the horse and make the same checks you made on the first side, from croup to withers to hooves.

By this time, you'll have a very good idea of the basic condition of your prospective purchase and should have been told its age. If no papers are presented, you'll have to check the age yourself. In fact, even with papers, it's a good idea to do so. It takes quite some time to become extremely accurate at checking a horse's age by examining its teeth, but it's easily possible to tell the five-year-old from the ten-year-old or older horse.

Because a description is of only minimal help in checking a horse's teeth, we've enclosed some drawings that will be of help. With the first-horse desirable age ranging from about nine years and up, those of greatest interest will be pictures of the incisors of a nine-year-old horse on through the eighteen-year-old. The others are helpful for comparison, as you can more easily tell what has been worn away if you know what was there in the first place.

To check the teeth, simply lift the horse's lip and use a finger of two in the gap you'll find (this is the spot where the bit

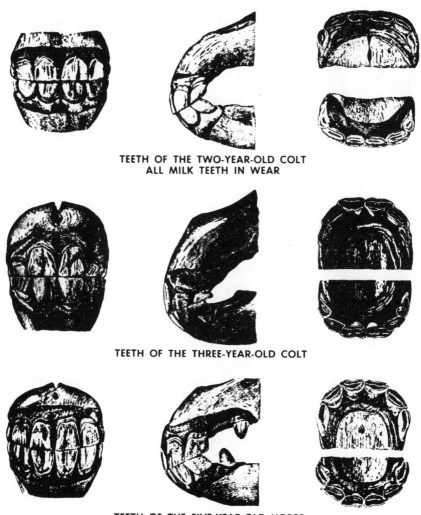

**TEETH OF THE TWO-YEAR-OLD COLT
ALL MILK TEETH IN WEAR**

TEETH OF THE THREE-YEAR-OLD COLT

TEETH OF THE FIVE-YEAR-OLD HORSE
Fig. 30. Teeth of two-, three-, and five-year-olds. Credit: 4-H.

normally rests) to open the mouth. Make your first check on the upper incisors. Though only one drawing shows it, and that faintly, Galvayne's grooves appear on the upper corner incisors starting at the age of ten. This groove will, on a twenty-year-old horse, extend the full length of the tooth, so that a horse with a Galvayne's groove halfway down its tooth will be just about

  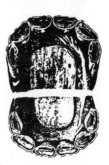

TEETH OF THE SEVEN-YEAR-OLD HORSE

TEETH OF THE TWELVE-YEAR-OLD HORSE

TEETH OF THE FIFTEEN-YEAR-OLD HORSE
Fig. 31. Teeth of seven-, twelve-, and fifteen-year-olds. Credit: 4-H.

TEETH OF THE TWENTY-ONE-YEAR-OLD HORSE
Fig. 32. Teeth of a twenty-one-year-old horse. Credit: 4-H.

fifteen years old. Oddly enough, at about twenty, the groove begins to disappear, at the gum line, and, should the horse live to such a ripe old age, will be totally gone by thirty.

The lower incisors start to show what are known as dental stars at about eight years of age; these start to show first on the lower central and intermediate pairs of teeth. Upper incisors will start to show dental stars at nine years, and all incisors will have them by age ten. By about twelve years of age, the dental stars will move from the front edges of the incisors back toward the centers of the teeth.

An experienced horseman can often tell within about a year or two just how old a horse is from its teeth, but some factors can cause premature wear. Horses that have been raised on sandy pasture will show greater tooth age than their real age.

After the list of possible catastrophes and so on, buying a horse may seem something no one with any sense would do. Unfortunately, almost any book on horses has to emphasize a great many unpleasant aspects so that a realistic view of the *possibilities* of horse ownership can be seen. These possibilities often read like a directory to Dante's Inferno, while in real life owning a horse is usually a great pleasure, with a measure of difficulty tossed in to keep us honest and alert.

While getting a veterinarian to check your prospective purchase may seem a good idea to many, and may well be many times, you can run into problems. If the vet is local, and you're not, the horse owner will exert more influence than you will and the vet will probably be reluctant to take on the job of judging the horse for you. If he should undertake the job and the sale isn't made, the seller will most likely blame the veterinarian.

When looking at a prospective horse, it's probably wiser to take an expert horseman with you if you happen to know one. If not, learn as much as you possibly can before trying to select your own horse, and make a list of the desirable features you are looking for and the things you will not, or cannot, accept. Blemishes are relatively unimportant, as their greatest effect is on appearance, but other faults need to be recognized. Too many people with too little experience buy horses. Learn to judge points on a variety of horses of different breeds, if at all possible. This follows a strong recommendation by almost all expert riders that the beginner ride as many horses as possible, as quickly as possible. Breadth of experience gives you a much stronger idea of the individuality of horses, and quickly helps you gain skill, whether the skill is in riding or selecting horses.

Some people select horses by color, wanting to match equipment, or simply having a liking for a particular color horse. I'm not all that choosy, but for some reason I do seem to prefer a buckskin, while a friend of mine has to have a bay or brown horse. It's mostly personal preference if the horse is suitable in other ways.

Horses come in a fairly wide variety of colors, with varied patterns of white at different spots. Most experts list five colors, with five major variations on those colors. The bay horse is a mixture of red and yellow, but may include many shades from a light, yellowish tan (light bay), to the dark bay with its rich-looking, near-brown coat. Usually the mane and tail will be black, and some points will also be black, though you will often see some white points.

The black horse is all black from muzzle to flanks, including the mane and tail. Dark browns and blacks are easily confused, but a check of the fine hairs at the muzzle and the flank hair should show no tan or brown hairs if the horse is a true black.

The brown horse is almost black, but has tan or brown hairs at the muzzle and flanks.

Chestnuts are basically red in color, with a shade variation

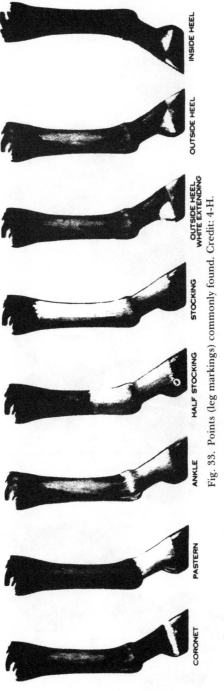

Fig. 33. Points (leg markings) commonly found. Credit: 4-H.

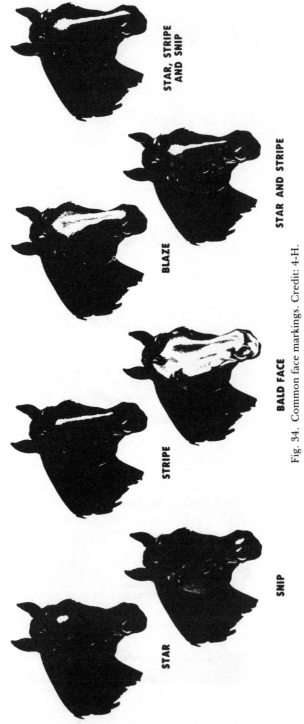

Fig. 34. Common face markings. Credit: 4-H.

from very light to a dark color almost like raw beef liver. There are many shades in between, including reddish gold and coppery shades. The mane and tail of a chestnut will be about the same shade as the body, or it will be a lighter, often a flaxen, color. If the tail is black, the horse is not a chestnut. This reddish color is also called sorrel.

White horses, true white horses, are born white and stay white throughout their lives. The hairs will be snowy white, the skin pink, and the eyes most often will be brown, though you may find the rare white horse with blue eyes.

The buckskin, or dun, horse is a yellowish color, and is the first of the major color variations. The color may range from a very pale yellow to a much darker yellow, always with a stripe down the back for a true dun. The dun may also have stripes on its legs. The mouse dun is the basic dun color imposed on any of the darker basic colors so that the coat has a smoky look. The buckskin dun is actually a dun color on a light bay coat, and the claybank dun is the basic yellow over or on a light chestnut or sorrel.

The gray horse has a mixture of white and black hairs, and the coat will lighten with age. Most grays are born nearly pure black and lighten gradually, some becoming almost snow white by four years of age.

The palomino is about the color of a gold coin, with a very light colored mane and tail in the white to ivory color range. Points and face markings are white.

The pinto is also called a calico or paint horse, and has irregularly spaced colored areas interspersed with white. Piebald pintos are black and white, while skewbald horses are white and any color other than black.

Roans are a mixture of white hairs with one or more darker base colors. A red roan mixes white with bay, while a strawberry roan is chestnut and white. A blue roan is a mixture of white and black hairs.

Points, or leg markings, and face markings are often important in identifying horses individually. The leg markings include a coronet, ankle pastern, and half and full stockings. Face markings are basic, but can be found in combination. A snip is a marking down between the nostrils, while a star is a marking up between the eyes. A stripe is just that, a wide marking that is thin and runs down the face. A blaze is a wider stripe, while the bald face is almost entirely white.

We hope that from this information and some gathered later in the book you'll at least be able to make a good start toward purchasing the perfect first horse for you. Of course, no perfect horses exist, but the closer you can come, the happier you'll be—even though the first horse for the novice rider must be a compromise no matter the amount of money and time spent looking animals over. If you keep riding, it won't be long before you'll want more than your first horse can possibly give, and you will then become a horse seller yourself. Proper riding and care of the horse during its life with you will help the animal to hold its value over the time you keep it.

Breed Associations

Appaloosas

Appaloosa Horse Club
P. O. Box 8403
Moscow, Idaho 83843

Colorado Ranger Horse Assoc.
John Morris, Pres.
7023 Eden Mill Rd.
Woodbine, Maryland 21797

Arabians

International Arabian Horse Assoc.
P. O. Box 4502
Burbank, California 91503

Half-Arab & Anglo-Arab Registries
P. O. Box 4502
Burbank, California 91503

Palominos

Palomino Horse Breeders of America
P. O. Box 249
Mineral Wells, Texas 76067

Palomino Horse Assoc., Inc.
P. O. Box 324
Jefferson City, Missouri

Paso

American Paso Fino Horse Assoc., Inc.
P. O. Box 2363
Pittsburgh, Pennsylvania 15230

Paso Fino Owners and Breeders Assoc., Inc.
P. O. Box 1579
Tryon, North Carolina 28782

Pintos

American Paint Horse Assoc.
P. O. Box 18519
Fort Worth, Texas 76118

Pinto Horse Assoc. of America, Inc.
7525 Mission Gorge Rd.
Suite C
San Diego, California 92120

Quarter Horses

American Quarter Horse Assoc.
Amarillo, Texas 79168

Standard Quarter Horse Assoc.
4390 Fenton St.
Denver, Colorado 80212

General Horses

American Bay Horse Assoc.
P. O. Box 884
Wheeling, Illinois 60090

American Buckskin Registry Assoc., Inc.
P. O. Box 1125
Anderson, California 96007

American Indian Horse Registry Assoc., Inc.
Geraldine Kluth, Pres.
1465 N. Valley Dr., Rt. 9
Apache Junction, Arizona 85220

American Morgan Horse Assoc., Inc.
Oneida Cty. Airport Industrial Park
P. O. Box 1
Wetmoreland, New York 13490

American Mustang Assoc., Inc.
P. O. Box 338
Yucaipa, California 92399

American Saddlebred Pleasure Horse Assoc.
Mrs. Joe Jackson, Secty./Treas.
P. O. Box 268
Columbus, Kansas 66725

Missouri Fox Trotting Horse Assoc.
P. O. Box 637
Ave, Missouri 65608

Morab Horse Registry of America
P. O. Box 143
Clovis, California 93612

Racking Horse Breeders' Assoc. of America
Helena, Alabama 35080

Spanish-Barb Breeders Assoc.
Peg Freitag, Secty.
P. O. Box 7479
Colorado Springs, Colorado 80933

Spanish Mustang Registry, Inc.
Jim Babbit, Secty./Treas.
Rt. 4, Box 64
Council Bluffs, Iowa 51501

Tennessee Walking Horse Breeders' & Exhibitors Assoc.
P. O. Box 286
Lewisburg, Tennessee 37091

Ponies

American Connemara Pony Society
Mrs. John O'Brien, Secty.
Rt. 1
Hosiekon Farm
Goshen, Connecticut 06756

American Quarter Pony Assoc.
Harold Wymore, Secty.
New Sharon, Iowa 50207

American Shetland Pony Club
P. O. Box 468
Fowler, Indiana 47944

National Appaloosa Pony, Inc.
Eugene Hayden, Exec. Secty.
P. O. Box 206
Gaston, Indiana 47342

National Quarter Pony Assoc.
Rt. 1
Marengo, Ohio 43334

Pony of the Americas Club, Inc.
P. O. Box 1447
Mason City, Iowa 50401

Welsh Pony Society of America
Gail Headley Hamilton, Secty.
P. O. Drawer A
White Post, Virginia 22663

While the above list is not complete, it covers most of the horses and ponies that will be of interest to the Western rider.

There seems little point in including the addresses of draft horse associations, nor of such groups as the American Hackney Horse Society. That is no reflection on the groups, nor on the animals they represent, simply a recognition of the fact that their purposes are not ours.

3. SADDLE UP
AND RIDE

Now we start moving into the actual riding part of Western horsemanship. Flop a saddle on the old mare's back and go. Well, not quite.

Saddling a horse requires a distinct procedure, and no ride of any duration at all should ever be made until you have carried out the steps needed to assure the saddle fits the horse as well as possible and is placed so that it won't gall the animal's back.

As a start, brush the back where the saddle will be placed, removing any loose hair and dirt. Start with a rubber currycomb, and finish with either a grooming glove or your bare hand, sweeping the hair and dirt to the horse's rump with the final strokes. The currycomb is used in small circles, with a fair amount of pressure. Most horses enjoy this particular part of preparation, as this is part of the area where horses, in herds, will groom each other.

Now the saddle blanket or pad is set in place, several inches forward of its final resting position. The spot, the exact spot, where a saddle is placed will vary a few inches from horse to horse, but generally start with the blanket well up over the withers, possibly even over the last hairs of the mane. Smooth the blanket carefully, making sure it is even on both sides of the horse and that there are no folds or creases to cut into the back. Use special care on saddle blankets that fold, as these can sneak

Fig. 35. This is how your saddle will be arranged before you start to lower it on the horse's back. All the rigging is kept on the near side to keep it from flopping down and causing the horse to shy.

a crease in on the underfold. Now, slide the saddle blanket back an inch or two so that the hairs of the back are smoothed in the right direction.

Pick up the saddle, making sure the offside (right) rigging and stirrup are either placed or tied so that they won't flop down on your horse's side. Basically, the idea is simply to prevent startling the horse while saddling him. If you make the job as pleasant as possible for the horse, you'll end up having less difficulty doing the saddling. Now, sit the saddle gently in place; don't lift the saddle and drop it in place, for even the lightest Western saddle will weigh upwards of twenty-four pounds, and no animal enjoys having that kind of weight dropped on its back. The saddle, like the blanket, goes a few inches further forward than its final position. It should center on the blanket, and, once the saddle is on the horse's back, be slipped back the final couple of inches to its proper spot. Once there, reach under the pommel and pull the blanket up a bit so it doesn't bind on the withers.

Now check again to see that the blanket is smooth, and lower the offside rigging and stirrup. Hang the left stirrup over the saddle horn, and reach under the horse's belly to pick up

Fig. 36. In this photo, I'm using a coarse brush to get Patches ready for her saddle, as she's just had a currycomb run over the area. This is a bit forward of actual saddle placement, but the blanket will start here and be pulled back, so dirt must be cleaned from the area.

Fig. 37. Tony Crilley sets a saddle blanket in place on Dividend.

Fig. 38. Note how far up on the neck Tony has placed the blanket. From here, it is pulled back into the correct spot.

Fig. 39. Tony starts to lower the saddle.

Fig. 40. The saddle is *lowered*, not dropped.

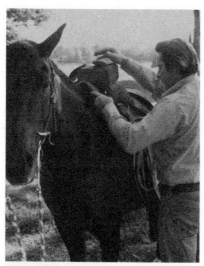

Fig. 41. The blanket or pad is pulled up into the gullet of the saddle to allow air to flow.

Fig. 42. Make sure there is plenty of space under the blanket, as it squashes down when the saddle is cinched.

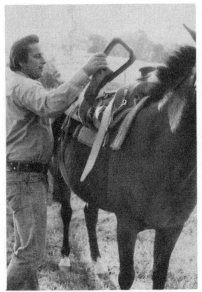

Fig. 43. Walk around to the offside of your horse and lower the stirrup and rigging instead of just flopping it over.

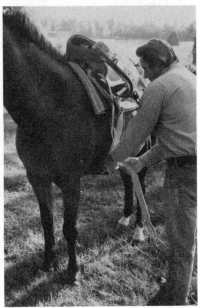

Fig. 44. The front latigo and cinch are fastened first.

Fig. 45. With the stirrup over the saddle horn, you've got plenty of room to work when pulling the latigo tight.

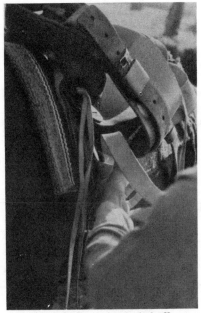

Fig. 46. The latigo is tied off.

Fig. 47. The front cinch should be about one hand behind the elbow. As a not so incidental point, before cinching your horse make sure the area covered by the cinch is clear of burrs, dirt, and debris.

the rigging straps. Bring the cinch under the belly and run the latigo strap through the cinch ring, drawing it up slowly. Pull the latigo through the cinch ring, drawing it up slowly. Pull the latigo through the cinch ring at least one more time and tie it off. Check to see if the belly has wrinkles, and try to tell if the horse has swelled its belly while being cinched. Wrinkles can often be removed simply by picking up the left front foot and pulling it forward a foot or so and then the right. If the belly appears to have swelled, lead the horse in a circle for a few steps and retighten the latigo strap. In fact, it's generally a good idea to lead the horse a bit and check the cinch whenever you saddle up.

The flank girth is fastened last. Each expert rider has a slightly different distance they prefer between flank girth and belly, but they are agreed it should never be more than a couple of inches, nor should it be tight on the horse before you mount. A too-tight flank girth is uncomfortable for the horse, while a too-loose one may allow the animal to get a hind foot caught. Either way, you could end up on the ground.

After saddling and checking the security of the rig, you'll need to bridle the horse. Usually, a horse is in a halter while being saddled so that it can be tied during the process. Never

Fig. 48. Fasten the rear rigging last.

Fig. 49. Lifting the front hoof and pulling a bit—gently—will remove belly wrinkles around and under the cinch. Do both legs.

Fig. 50. Dividend, alert and ready to go.

Fig. 51. The halter is slipped back over the neck, as Jim Shands is doing here, before bridling the horse.

Fig. 52. Use the left hand to hold the headstall at the top.

tie a horse with the reins because this can damage its mouth should it pull back.

Slip the halter back over the horse's neck, making sure it is not totally free in case he objects to being bitted. With your right hand place the headstall up between the ears, holding the bit in your left hand. Use your fingers to pull the curb strap back out of the way and guide the bit mouthpiece into the horse's mouth and between the teeth.

Some horses take bitting more readily than do others, but if the horse doesn't want to take the bit, using the above method, your left thumb is in a position to slip along the lips and slide into the area where there are no teeth. A slight pressure there will most always cause the horse to open up for bitting. Trying to ram the bit mouthpiece into the mouth is liable to do nothing more than contribute to making the horse harder than ever to bit the next time you get ready to ride.

A few considerations are also in order. If you're getting ready to ride on a cold day, you should hold the bit in your hand, inside your jacket, or some other warm place, so that it has time to warm up before being inserted in your horse's mouth. Icy metal being stuck in the mouth is the cause of more than one horse that's usually easy to bit becoming recalcitrant.

Fig. 53. The headstall is carried up over the forelock, as shown.

Fig. 54. Patches thinks she's being maligned, or would if she could reason as we do. She's an exceptionally easy-to-handle mare, even for her young age (4½), so slipping a thumb into the bars usually isn't necessary.

Fig. 55. The headstall is now slipped the rest of the way over the ears (in this case, one ear since it is a single ear headstall).

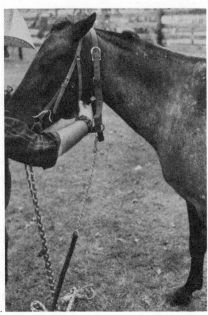

Fig. 56. The throatlatch is fastened.

All sorts of tricks are used to get a hard-to-bit horse to take the mouthpiece. Some people rub honey or molasses on the mouthpiece. Essentially, this will work, but it's a messy and somewhat bad practice. Generally, bitting the horse as gently as possible, using the thumb on the gums to provide slight pressure to open the mouth, works best.

It helps to make certain the bit fits the horse, too. A too-small mouthpiece is going to pinch (and some cheap bits with moveable cheekpieces will do the same, whether they fit or not: a bit is not a good place to economize), while a too-large bit will place pressure in the wrong spots. Most Western bits are curb style, and a curb bit that fits correctly will have the mouthpiece in contact with the corners of the horse's mouth. The curb strap or chain will be just loose enough under the jaw so that you can slip two fingers between it and the lower jaw.

Mechanical hackamores are usually used with curb straps or chains, and the measurement of distance is the same. True hackamores and bosals are more complex arrangements. Like the mechanical hackamore, these devices have rawhide portions that curve around the horse's nose, but these go down around the lower jaw and join in a ball-like heel knot. Mecate reins are tied to the heel knot, and the bosal or hackamore is attached to the regular headstall.

Hackamores exert pressure on the lower outside portion of the jawbones where the bone is covered with only a thin layer of flesh. Mechanical hackamores provide pressure on the nose, also covered with a thin layer of flesh, and the curb groove. The leverage factor applied by the long shanks on the mechanical hackamore (also called a hackamore bit by some) is great and requires careful use to prevent breaking through the skin in the sensitive areas.

A heavy hackamore of the regular type offers more than enough leverage for the ham-handed rider to damage the horse. As with all control devices, light hands are needed.

 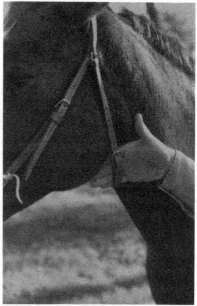

Fig. 57. Your horse is now bridled, bitted, and ready to go except for one last check. . . .

Fig. 58. The throatlatch should allow four fingers to slip in under the horse's neck.

Hackamores and bosals of whatever type should rest easy on the nose without putting undue pressure on nerves. A too-tight hackamore is a thing to be totally avoided.

Now, with the saddle on and secure, the bit in, and the reins attached, you still have the halter looped around the horse's neck. Leave it there for a moment and take time to make a rough check on the length of the stirrup leathers. This rough check has your hand (right hand for near side, left for offside) placed against the edge of the seat cover on the saddle, with the stirrup held up under your arm. The stirrup should snug just up under your arm on both sides. Generally, with factory-made saddles, you can go ahead and count the number of holes the near side stirrup leather is adjusted to and match them on the offside without measuring there. But it's best, with any saddle, to check the length between holes just in case the saddlemaker goofed and didn't get them equal. You can believe me when I say that unequal hanging stirrups are not the handiest thing to have should the horse be even a little frisky. And unequal stirrup lengths can ruin your balance in any type of riding.

If adjustments need to be made to equalize the stirrup length, you'll probably have to find someone who has shoe-maker's equipment, as normal leather punches won't cut through the heavy leather used in a saddle. Once the stirrup leathers are at the correct or near-correct length, you're ready to mount.

Mounting is a process that receives far too little attention when people are learning to ride. Many novice riders—and not a few near experts—do the job improperly, either dragging a foot along the horse's rump, grinding a pointed boot toe into the animal's side, or just about yanking the saddle from its moorings as they swing up.

Stand on the near side of your horse and face the saddle. Keep an eye on the animal's ears as you prepare to mount. Place your right hand on the saddle horn, and hold the reins in your left hand. The toe is placed in the stirrup, with the stirrup turned so your toe points to the front of the horse (this helps prevent that grinding-in motion that will make even the best-trained horse shy away during mounting). Facing the saddle,

Fig. 59. Tony prefers to use one hand on the cantle when mounting, but for most people it is best not to have to remove that hand to swing your leg over.

and getting that toe in the boot are important, for now, should the horse try to shy to the front, you're in a position to go ahead and use its momentum to swing you into the saddle. It's best, though, to use the reins to check the horse, for any well-trained horse should stand steady for mounting. You're in a position to more easily check the horse's indicators—its ears— to see if it's about to move. The ears will tell you a lot more about what the horse is going to do than will any other body clues.

As you prepare to mount, the reins are in the left hand, with which you should now reach up and clutch some of the mane, just forward of the saddle. You can also hold onto the saddle gullet at the pommel if you want. The reins are held just tightly enough to keep the horse in place. Too-loose reins may allow the horse to move before you're ready, while keeping the reins too tight can cause the animal to back up.

With all else in position we come to the part where most beginning riders make a mistake. You have one hand gripping the reins and the mane and the other gripping the saddle horn. It may seem sensible to go ahead and push up with the left leg, while pulling yourself into the saddle, but it is incorrect, can

Figs. 60 and 61. The right leg provides the spring when mounting, *not* the left leg.

pull the saddle awry, and can cause the horse to shy. Use the muscles of the right leg to push your body up over the saddle, with most of your body weight coming over the saddle, not on the left stirrup. Swing the right leg over the horse smoothly, making sure it's high enough not to bump the horse's rump (another time the horse may start to move out before you're completely mounted).

When you settle into the saddle, do it gently. This goes back to not dropping the saddle on the horse. Even a light rider is likely to weigh 100 or more pounds, and in my case dropping 200 or more pounds from a foot or so in the air onto the horse's back is just plain unneeded and a bit cruel. It may take you a bit of time to learn to balance with one leg in the stirrup and the other swinging free on the opposite side of your horse, but this skill will come with a bit of practice.

Get your right foot in the right stirrup as quickly as possible (later on, I'll cover the methods of setting a saddle up so the stirrups point correctly for this: as they're delivered, stirrups

Fig. 62. The upper body quickly swings over the horse's centerline, as the leg goes high enough to clear the rump.

Fig. 63. Tony settles gently into the saddle, not just flopping into place.

Fig. 64. Ready to go. Note Dividend's ears as she keeps alert to Tony's cues.

are tricky things to get your feet into because of the angle at which they hang).

The fit of the saddle is important to you. Most people riding Western saddles take a fifteen-inch seat, but there is a variation from child's saddles on up past sixteen inches in some custom-made models. My own saddle has a 15½-inch seat. The seat should fit well without forcing you to sit up over the cantle or providing you with too much slipping and sliding room.

Stirrups should be adjusted so that, with your feet in the stirrup to the ball of the foot, standing places your tail about one hand's depth (flat) out of the saddle. Keep your heels down. Place the reins in whichever hand you prefer (if this is your first ride and the horse isn't trained to neck rein, you'll probably want one rein in each hand). Your back is kept straight—horseback riding is an excellent way to improve posture. Your hips will be just over the middle of the saddle. This allows your weight to be carried by your pelvic structure instead of placing it on the buttocks.

Fig. 65. The heels are kept down, and you ride on the balls of your feet.

You should, if your seat is correct, find your thighs slanting down and forward at about a forty-five-degree angle, with your feet also about forty-five degrees from the parallel line of the horse. Below the knee, your legs will make slight contact with the horse, with the inside of both calves and knees resting easily and gently against the stirrup leathers. In Western riding, leg grip is seldom used, as the seat is supposed to be balanced. You should be riding on the balls of your feet and using your legs to cushion any shock.

Decide which hand is to be the bridle hand (the hand holding the reins): the left is probably most common. Carry the reins forward in the right hand, keeping the back of your hands pointed toward the horse's ears and the fingers pointed down. For single hand reining, place the ring finger of your left hand between the reins, or use the index finger if you wish. Make sure the reins are of equal length, and slide the left hand forward of the saddle coming to a stop a few inches in front of the saddle horn. The ends of the reins will now come out between forefinger and thumb and will fall to the right of the horse's neck. Turn your hand so the little finger is down.

The wrist should be flexed and a bit curved, so that now you have light contact with your horse's mouth. Keep your elbow just touching your side, and keep your forearm just about parallel with the ground. The elbow should be in a straight line with the bit, and must remain there as you change the position of the reins.

Western riding is done with reins that appear to be, and are, slightly slack. The contact with your horse's mouth is minimal, and very light. This is probably the hardest of all techniques for the novice to learn, and the reason why I have gone into such detail. The only cure for heavy hands is a lot of thought and practice. In time, light hands will come naturally—but only with time. You will also learn that no matter what happens on that horse you do not use the reins to keep your balance. Sawing at the reins in such a manner only makes a bad situation worse. If you can't keep your balance, grab the saddle horn, but never, ever use the reins for such.

Your first rides shouldn't be at speeds that will cause you to be in danger of losing your balance anyway. They should, if at all possible, take place in a moderate-sized enclosure, such as a corral or riding ring. Keep the horse at a walk until you feel secure, and then a few days past that time, and you'll pick up all the necessary skills quickly. One friend, who rides exceptionally well, recommends at least a week of riding in an enclosure, supplemented by a couple of hours each day riding easy trails at a walk. During this time, he goes along—unaccompanied rides by inexpert riders is a good way to get hurt, and a poor way to learn as there is no one to correct your mistakes, should you miss noticing them yourself.

The trail riding can continue at a walk for as long as the individual takes to get accustomed to the skills needed for faster riding. There is little difference in technique for fast riding and slow riding, especially in the all-important areas of handling the reins and keeping the body in balance, so these skills can be learned as well, and much more safely, at a walk.

There are walks and walks, of course. We've all seen the rental stable plug that won't go at better than a plod no matter how hard you cue it. Then we look at the alert horse under a good horseman and see it walk with almost twice the action and speed.

As you start the horse forward, slack off pressure on your reins to the point where you can just barely feel the horse's mouth at all. Adding pressure will cause many horses to back up when they get leg cues. Squeeze your legs against the horse's sides as you slack off on the rein pressure, tightening the pressure gently, and the horse should move off.

If the horse doesn't move off with a good squeeze, kick his sides with your heels. Some horses are trained to accept this cue, rather than the squeeze. If neither works, go back to zero, using the reins to get his attention. Tighten up a bit, but don't jerk or saw—so that you have a bit more mouth feel—and relax any cueing. Go back, then, to the slack-rein cue and give the horse a well-defined kick in each side. Once the horse begins to move forward, stop the cueing whether you're squeezing or kicking.

As the horse moves, the insides of your thighs, your knees, and the upper part of your calves will be against the horse (or saddle, actually). No pressure is used here. Keep your body inclined slightly forward; at the same time maintain a straight, or even slightly convex, back. Your body should move with the horse, and your hands and wrist holding the reins will give to the motions of the horse's head. You should keep a constant, steady, and light mouth contact without alternating between tight and slack reins, which only serves to confuse the horse.

With the ball of your foot in the stirrup, allow your ankles to flex in time with the horse's motion, at the same time keeping your heels down. Your waist will be relaxed, flexing with the animal's movements.

Every expert I've ever talked to or read recommends the novice horseman ride as many horses as possible. The rationale is an excellent one, given the individuality of horses. Each horse reacts differently to the same cues, though the differences may sometimes be barely apparent even to a skilled eye. One horse may move out promptly on the correct cues, while

Fig. 66. Poor Dividend. She's almost asleep, or so it seems. Note, though, that her ears are turned back to Tony as he starts the spring for a bareback mount.

Fig. 67. Tony quickly gets his body weight over the horse, using both hands to assist his spring.

another may need a firm boot in the ribs to get it stepping. Another may overreact to the cues, bursting into a trot from a standstill (try to avoid this kind of horse until you've had quite a few hours in the saddle). Each has a slightly different cadence at different gaits. If you are to become an accomplished horseman, you must learn to adjust to the differing requirements that such individuality presents.

Now with all the detail we've gone into to get you saddled, bridled, and finally at a walk on a horse, you may begin to wonder if it's all worth it. Each person makes his or her own decision on that, naturally, but consider the detail as something that takes only a short time to learn. It doesn't have to be learned over and over again. Once you've learned to saddle and mount properly, the steps will flow one into another, as the steps in cueing the horse and maintaining a proper seat will flow as you practice. And the practice itself can be fun, especially once you're out of an enclosure and riding trails, pasture, or other, more open, areas.

The process of learning to ride is an extensive one, though: becoming a good rider takes a lot of time, energy, and work.

Fig. 68. The right leg comes up and over, while the reins are held in case checking is needed. Note that Dividend's eyes are again half-closed, though the ears remain alert to the motion on her back. Bareback mounting is nothing new to her, as Tony's daughter Jodi frequently rides her that way.

Figs. 69 and 70. Wriggling into position requires a bit more work, and a steady horse is a big help. Note that as Tony approaches the final spot, Dividend is totally alert and ready.

Once you've gotten used to keeping your balance on a saddle, you've reached the time to try riding bareback to further develop your control skills and balance. (Some experts feel that every rider should start on a bareback animal, but I tend to feel that some semblance of control is a better thing to bring to a horse being so ridden, particularly since the processes of mounting and staying on are a bit more difficult.)

Mounting the bareback horse requires, first, a horse that will either stand still quite readily, or one that is easily checked with the reins the instant it begins to move. By the time you've mounted a few times with a saddle, you'll have an idea of how your horse is likely to behave in such a situation, but because the techniques are different, you can't be absolutely sure.

Bridle the horse, and hold the reins in the left hand, as with a saddled mount. Place your left hand at the base of the mane, and face the horse. Use your legs for spring, signal the horse—whatever voice signal you use—and spring onto its back, getting as much of your upper body weight as possible across the back, up as close to the withers, as you can. Use your right and left hands to assist in getting the needed amount of spring, though be careful not to haul back on the reins, causing the animal to back up. If you've started the mount properly, your stomach will be over the horse's back, just behind the withers (as an incidental, this is a good time to remove that large belt buckle, for a gouged horse is a moving horse: my own thoughtlessness in this area a couple of weeks ago nearly ended up with me sprawled on my face). If your horse starts to move once you're across his back, you can use the reins to check him.

Now, lift your right knee, give your shoulders a twist and, helping with your hands, swing gently into position. Check the horse with the reins and slip up to the correct bareback-riding position, just as close to the withers as you can get without actually being on them. Keep your back straight, as in saddle riding, but get a good leg grip with your thighs, calves, and heels, keeping the heels locked in close to the horse just behind its elbows. Again, the heels, though in and locked, are kept down, so that the toe is a bit higher and pointed slightly outward.

Fig. 71. Jodi takes Dividend for a bit of a ride, bareback. Note how far forward she is seated, and note the relatively taut ·reins (for Western riding). Dividend had never had this particular bit, nor anything like it, in her mouth before, having been raised and trained on a D-ring snaffle. Trammel makes an almost straight bar curb bit with a copper mouthpiece, and that's what I had with me this day.

Sitting a horse bareback, and riding at a walk, is one thing. Riding the same way at a trot, something you may easily find yourself doing if you ever enter a Western show with a bareback-riding class, is a bit more of a chore, and may be done most easily on those horses having a smoother trot. This gait tends to choppiness anyway and can make keeping one's grip and balance difficult. A walk is a natural gait, and a four-beat one. A horse with a good walk will have a springy and regular stride, so balance is easily maintained. A walk is also the slowest gait. A trot is a seminatural gait (the walk and the gallop are the primary natural gaits), and works on a two-beat diagonal—a front foot and the opposite hind foot take off at the same time and strike the ground at the same time. Different horses can vary widely in the smoothness of this gait, and it's hard to judge just how a horse will go until you've ridden it at the trot.

For a fact, though, learning to sit a trot smoothly while bareback will improve your saddle riding immeasurably, for a sure sign of a novice rider is slackness in the saddle at the trot.

As another incidental, you *can* post while riding a Western saddle, but most riders who post do so with such a very slight body rise that it is just about impossible to note. Still, if the horse is a rough trotter, even the top rider is going to be, and look, uncomfortable. If you wish to try posting (with a saddle: again, posting can even be done bareback, but it takes an immense amount of strength in thighs and calves), for whatever reason—generally because the horse is rough at the trot—start by rising with, for example, the left front hoof for a short time. If, after a few minutes, you shift off and post while the right hoof is rising, then you'll ease up on the horse a bit.

Once you start to become confident bareback, switch back and forth between saddled riding and bareback for a time. Keep all action at a trot or slower, and start keeping in mind the correct seat, the correct rein position and slackness or tautness, keeping your heels down, your back straight, your head up. Become aware of your horse's ear movement, for it can tell you much about the amount of attention the horse is paying you. As you cue the horse to move out, the ears should cock slightly back toward you as if the animal were awaiting a voice command. (Almost everyone uses voice commands with horses these days, but it is considered impolite to cluck at your horse during shows, as you may cue another person's horse and spoil the chances of that rider. In fact, voice cues are sometimes considered not overly polite when riding in any sort of company, as a few horses will move out on anyone's cue.)

Oddly enough, the trot will seem the hardest gait to master, for even though the canter and lope (a Western adaptation of the canter, at a slower pace) are related to the gallop, they are smoother, and not much, if any, faster than the trot.

Working at the canter requires more knowledge on the part of the rider, for it is a three-beat gait that places extra wear on the leading forefoot and its diagonal hindfoot. It is at this point that you begin to learn something of changing leads. What you learn here will also serve you well at a gallop, for that is another gait at which lead changes are needed. The change of leads not only evens out the extra wear caused by these gaits, it provides greater support in turns. For example, if a horse goes into a turn with the outside legs leading, you, and the horse, may be in trouble, as the animal has very little support on the side where it is most needed.

A description of the sequence in which a cantering horse's hooves strike the ground may help in understanding just what leads are. In the left lead, the right hind leg touches first, then the left hind leg, followed almost instantly by the right foreleg, then the left foreleg will strike and the beat sort of pauses as all four hooves are off the ground for an instant. In a collected canter, the shoulder will also lead, for as the left hind leg leads the right in a left lead, the left shoulder should also lead the right. As a start, you'll probably have to peer down at your horse's feet to tell what lead it's in. To check, horses in the left lead will have the left forefoot go further out than the right, while a horse in a right lead will have the right foreleg or foot further out. You should get away from the need for peering down at the feet as soon as possible, and the easiest way to do this is to begin to feel how your body responds to the leads. Check the horse's feet and then check your feet. Your left foot will move ahead when the horse is on the left lead, and vice versa for the right lead. Now, after a time you won't have to look at all, for you'll gain enough knowledge of body position and feel for the movement of your horse to realize that you're in the correct, or incorrect, lead.

Some beginners' horses are what is called one-leaded. This is not too handy, as you'll often need to change leads to get support in turns; as you continue riding you'll be making sharper and faster turns where getting as much support under the horse as possible can prevent a spill. If the horse has been ridden for too long by novices, though, it may well refuse to change from, say, a right lead, into a left lead. Basically, what you'll need to do, assuming you're able to correctly identify the leads, is to trot the horse in a small circle to the left. Keep increasing the speed of the trot until the horse breaks into the correct lead. Once the horse starts going into the correct lead, you'll need to spend several days reinforcing this bit of retraining, though the time will vary with your riding ability and just how badly the horse was allowed to drop one lead. Keep the animal training until it easily takes the lead change and you should have few problems.

Actually, much of the time it's the rider who has the most difficulty with lead changes. Once you've learned to recognize the lead your horse is in, you need to learn to make flying lead changes. Start by learning the correct cues for a lead change, and then learn when to apply those cues. The cues will vary depending on who trained your horse, as some trainers work with nothing more than cueing the horse with the leg in the direction you wish it to go, picking up on the reins and neck reining the horse in the correct direction. Others add a slight shift of body weight, though any lean should be just about negligible. You have to stay on top of your horse if you're to keep balance in the saddle.

There are only two times to cue a horse for a lead change. The back feet must be on the ground, or the lead foot must be in the air. Use the leg cue as the lead foot is in the air: rein the horse as soon as the lead foot touches the ground. It takes time to do this smoothly, but in a short time it will come easily and the lead changes will be smooth and nearly imperceptible. The first cue, the leg cue, lets the horse know something is coming, while the second cue is the performance cue. You've given him an instant to get ready, and a well-trained horse will immediately shift into the correct lead.

Once the riding is completed, you're ready to unsaddle and begin caring for your horse. Proper unsaddling is a must, as is dismounting. Swinging down off a horse, the reins are held as they were in mounting, with the hand at the base of the mane, and, if you wish, grasping some mane, while the right hand is on the saddle horn. Make sure the left leg clears the rump as you swing it back, and try to make the dismount one smooth move, putting as little weight on one side of the horse as possible. Also, keep that left toe pointed to the front! Getting off a shying horse, one just gouged in the ribs with a pointed boot toe, is no more fun than mounting one. The reins should be held as in mounting, with just enough mouth contact to keep the horse in place, yet not so much it starts to back up on you.

Removing the saddle starts with the rear girth, which is unbuckled and is left to hang for a minute. Untie the front girth latigo, and move around to the offside and lift the offside stirrup and girths onto the saddle. Now, come around and lift the saddle off your horse. Slide the blanket off.

Check for dry spots and signs of soreness. Give the horse at least a quick brushing where the saddle was, and use an old towel to dry him down where the blanket rested. If the horse is very sweaty, you may wish to use a sweat scraper to get the heaviest accumulation off. If the day is chilly and the horse is sweaty, he should be dried and then walked to cool him off. Don't water a hot horse, as that can founder the animal. Instead, walk him for several minutes (at least fifteen), and then let the animal drink sparingly, walking it for several more minutes before allowing another sip.

Such treatment will take some time, but helps prevent problems which can add to pain, expense, and lost time overall, so is well worth the effort involved.

At this point in the rider's and horse's day, some special handling and care for the animal, over and above the basic cooling out and watering and wiping down, may well make for a closer bond between horse and rider. A check of the horse, and some more extensive grooming, will provide a reward for the animal and pleasure for the horseman as the day nears its end. For that reason, before we go on to details of more advanced riding, our next chapter will cover grooming.

4. CARING FOR YOUR HORSE

C are of the horse is basic in the prevention of many sorts of difficulties. It should start with a good grooming each day, or as often as possible, a check of the hooves, and shoes—if used—before and after each ride, and includes the general management of the healthy horse's activities. Nutrition is especially important, and will be dealt with in a separate chapter, for the horse is in some ways easier to feed than some other animals, while being more sensitive to dietary changes than most.

Basic care starts with the horse's feet. The old horseman's adage of "no hoof, no horse" is still true and is likely to remain so. The structure of the hoof is a marvel of complexity, and also of strength, considering the job it is so often asked to do today. Many of us ride on hard surfaces, and it has been estimated that a moderate-size horse carrying a rider and saddle on such a surface can induce a landing force in each hoof of about 10,000 foot-pounds each time it strikes the ground. Considering this, we sometimes have to wonder why, though hoof troubles just about lead the list of equine problems, there aren't more difficulties in this area. The structure of the hoof offers one explanation. Six major bones make up the internal structure of the hoof and lower leg; these bones—the cannon, splint, long pastern, short pastern, coffin, and navicular—slide over each other on natural cushions so that shock is absorbed when the hoof strikes. The hoof also spreads a bit on impact, absorbing more shock.

The cannon bone is a long bone, below the knee in a front leg (the hock in the rear leg). Splint bones attach to it as the horse grows; from this the long pastern and short pastern angle down to the coffin and navicular bones. The pastern bones are angled, as we said, and this angle determines the angle of the hoof, which varies a bit among horses, but normally will be about forty-five degrees. More important than the actual angle of the hoof or pastern is the need for those two to match angles. If corrective trimming is needed, then the angle may occasionally be changed by the farrier, but such work is avoided where possible.

The horny outside covering of the hoof, starting at the coronary band, is similar in construction to the material in our fingernails and is no more sensitive to trimming. Still, like our fingernails, too-close trimming will cause discomfort or even pain. And *only* the horny growth should be trimmed. This growth serves to enfold and protect the inner structures of the hoof and is the basic wearing surface of the hoof. Above this is the perioplic ring, the site of periople production. Periople is a natural varnishlike substance that covers the outer surface of the hoof and helps to prevent excessive dryness. The white line, when viewed from the bottom, lies just inside the horny wall of the hoof and is sensitive to pain: generally, the width is about an eighth of an inch, and serves as an indicator to the horseman, or farrier, as to the limits of shoeing. A nail driven inside the white line may well enter the sensitive structures of the hoof and cause lameness.

In the middle of the hoof, viewed from the bottom, is a V-shaped pad of material that feels horny to the touch. This is the frog; it compresses under weight before transmitting striking forces to other elastic structures in the hoof and is another aid to shock absorption. If problems with the frog's elasticity develop, they can allow the hoof to shrink and result in contracted feet and lameness. Around the frog are deep grooves known as commissures. These grooves provide the space into which the frog expands, so are also essential to healthy hooves.

parts of a horse

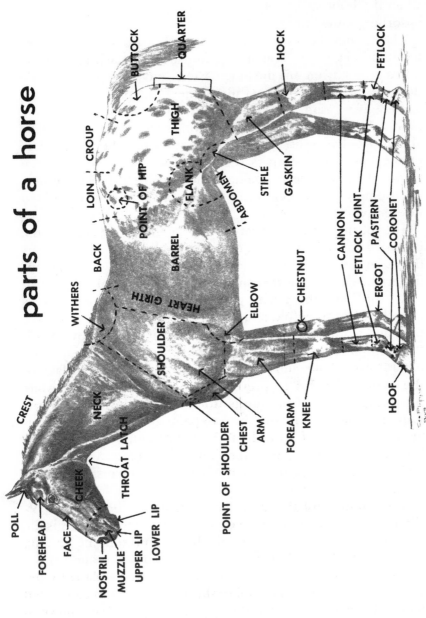

Fig. 72. Parts of a horse. Credit: Appaloosa Horse Club.

Fig. 73. The V shape formed by the frog is easily seen.

The sole of the hoof is a thick plate of horny material growing out from the internal fleshy sole; it serves to protect those inner structures, though it was not intended by nature to carry weight, as the wall and frog area are meant to do.

On an average, a hoof will grow a bit under half an inch a month, necessitating trimming and a regular check of shoes. Horse shoeing is considered by all horsemen to be a necessary evil for animals used on hard surfaces. If at all possible, a horse worked lightly, or kept on softer surfaces, should be trimmed periodically and left barefoot. The horseshoe acts to limit expansion of the hoof, and that expansion is an essential part of the built-in shock absorbing mechanism. With horseshoes, the frog can't contact the ground, so it isn't able to do its work as well, thus more shock is transmitted to the hoof, and the result can too often be a lamed horse.

Horseshoes, when needed, should be as thin as possible so that the frog has the greatest chance of contacting the ground. Not only do the shoes limit the work of the frog, but the nails driven through the walls make those walls more susceptible to cracking, while also limiting the opportunity the walls have to expand. All in all, if your horse is used primarily in sandy and other soft areas, leave it barefoot. If your horse has hard, thick walls on its hooves, then you can often leave it barefoot where another animal would need shoes. If your horse has thin, soft hoof walls, then you may need shoes even when conditions are ideal.

Generally, a horse with a broad, well-spread hoof, especially at the heel, will usually have fewer problems with hoof expansion, but may pull up lame from simple sole tenderness in rough country sooner than a horse with a more contracted and less ideal hoof. The reason: more small rocks contact the hard sole and cause soreness.

Hoof care for the Western rider begins with a daily check for cracks of any kind. Such a check requires a horse that will stand to allow you to lift its feet, for a simple gaze down only works to pick up the most obvious faults. You'll also want to lift the foot to check for thrush and bruises and to clean the hoof and make sure it is free of other problems around the sole area.

People differ in certain areas of lifting a foot to check a hoof, but the basics are similar. First, let the horse know what you're doing, gently and firmly. If you're preparing to check a front hoof, stand by the horse's shoulder, place your inside hand on the animal's shoulder and starting from there run your outside hand down the leg. Don't try, unless your horse is very well trained, to simply lift the leg by bending and tugging: although many horses will tolerate this, it's best to make the horse aware of what's to come. As your hand reaches the pastern, give a small push with the hand on the shoulder to get the horse to shift its weight to the opposite hoof, and, when your other hand reaches the fetlock, you'll usually have an easy job of lifting the hoof. For horses that won't lift the hoof, a gentle squeeze just above the fetlock will usually work.

If you're cleaning the hoof, put your inside shoulder into the horse's shoulder and use both hands on the hoof, starting from the heel with the hoof pick and working back to the toe.

To examine the hind feet, stand close to the horse, again

Fig. 74. Let the horse know what's coming when you get ready to lift its hoof.

Fig. 75. Keep a firm but gentle contact with the leg as you move your hand down.

Fig. 76. In most cases, if the horse is used to being handled, a simple tug will bring the leg up.

Fig. 77. Tip the toe up to make the check easier.

facing the rear. The inside hand is used at the hip or thigh to shift the horse's weight, while the outside hand moves down the leg to the top of the fetlock. After that, the procedure is the same as for a front hoof until the hoof comes off the ground, at which time you should place your inside knee against the cannon bone (the long bone below the hock), and take a small step forward. This will bring the leg and foot behind the horse and should effectively keep it from shifting weight onto you, also making it hard for the horse to draw its leg forward to kick. Don't go so far to the rear of the animal that you throw it off balance. The hoof will be easier to work on if you tip the toe up a little, too.

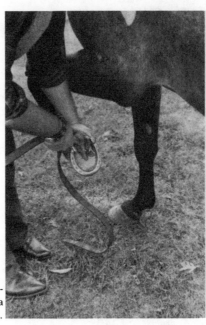

Fig. 78. Daily hoof cleaning is an important item of equine care, so having a hoof pick on hand is always a good idea.

Examine each hoof with care as you lift it, and as you hold it. Look for major cracks in all areas of the hoof wall, and check for shoe fit and loose nails if the horse is shod. Clean the hoof carefully with the pick and check around the frog for any acrid odor or pungent-smelling discharge. Thrush is the cause of this odor and must be treated immediately, as it can cause tissue deterioration and lameness. It is most often found in the hind feet, between the cleft of the frog, or in the commissure grooves. It is caused by a fungus, and needs, therefore, a fungicide, but the fungus develops because of filthy stabling habits. Keeping the horse in a clean, well-bedded stall will prevent thrush.

If a horse is confined to a stable for much of its life, it may also suffer from a condition known as dry hooves. If your horse's hooves appear dry and brittle (showing splits and cracks initially, after which the frogs may lose their elasticity, allowing them to shrink and the heels to contract, with a lamed horse as a result), a hoof dressing is probably needed. Horses kept in stables should have the hooves coated with hoof dressing each day. Coat the hoof from the coronary band down to the bottom of the horny wall, then coat, heavily, the underside of the hoof, including the frog. The bottoms of the feet should be cleaned before the dressing is applied, for most of the moisture in the hoof rises through the soles.

If cracks and splits, or other signs of hoof dryness, are excessive, have a farrier do any corrective trimming and shoeing needed before dressing the hooves.

A good farrier is needed for hoof care. Your farrier should be able to tell you under just what conditions a horse will need shoeing—be as accurate as possible when working out your riding plans, so you'll both have a fairly good picture of the kind of terrain you'll be riding over. He can also check and repair some hoof damage and indicate to you any special care you must provide the horse. He can do corrective trimming for some defects; in the case, for example, of the splayfooted horse (the front toes turn out with the heels turned in), the farrier will

Fig. 79. Patches stands steady while her hooves are sprayed with dressing; some horses won't. The hoof must also be lifted and the bottom cleaned and liberally coated with dressing.

trim the outer half of the hoof. Contracted heels are treated by first keeping the hoof moist, then by lowering the heels so that the frog carries more of the weight and spreads the heels further apart.

By doing daily hoof checks, and checking both before and after each ride, you keep a good watch on your animal's hoof condition, so that any problems are caught early, when they are more easily corrected. Uncorrected hoof problems can cause a lost horse.

BASIC GROOMING

Basic grooming differs from show grooming in several ways. The emphasis in basic grooming is to keep the animal as comfortable as possible in a more or less natural state; tail braiding and such are seldom bothered with outside the show ring. Since few, if any, Western classes require braiding the animal's mane and tail, we won't bother with that here, but some show grooming will be covered for those who are interested.

Grooming tools are all important to a good job. As a start, you'll need a good rubber currycomb, a mane and tail comb, a hoof pick, and a sweat scraper. Add an old towel and you're set to begin. For further work, you may wish to use a grooming mitt (a rubber mitt with raised nipples on it), a shedder/scraper for removing winter coats, and two grooming brushes, one moderately stiff and one fairly soft. Little else, beyond some shampoo formulated for the horse, a sponge, and a bucket, are needed for standard grooming—show grooming may require some coat conditioner.

The rubber currycomb is used to rough out the horse (you can also use a metal currycomb for this job) to remove caked sweat, dirt, and grime. Use a small circular motion on the areas where grime is heavy, and use a fair amount of strength (use less with the sharper-toothed metal currycombs). The hair is left roughed up. Neither metal nor rubber currycombs are ever used below the knees or hocks, nor are they used on the face. When one side of the horse is roughed up, move on to the

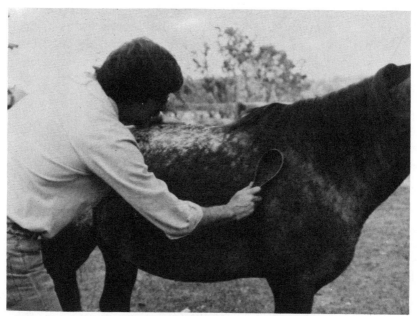

Fig. 80. Using a shedder/scraper to remove excess hair.

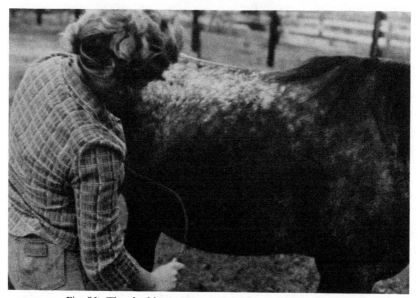

Fig. 81. The shedder/scraper can also be opened up for use.

other. When both sides are roughed up, pick up the stiffer of your two brushes and use it to brush the hair back down.

Horses are herd animals and, as such, groom themselves in certain areas, but the underbelly and cinch areas are not touched in this natural grooming. Such areas, varying from horse to horse as they do with humans, tend to be ticklish, and grooming here may cause even a well-trained horse to shy. Because of this a lot of people don't groom the underbelly and cinch areas as well as they should. These areas, especially after a wet ride, can become heavily caked with mud and sweat, and such debris under a cinch causes sores. If your horse won't stand easily for this part of the grooming, you will have to cross tie it, but don't avoid the areas.

A final finish after the brushing can be put on the horse by using either the flat of your hand, an old, soft towel, or the softer of your two brushes.

The areas below the knees and hocks are best cleaned with the grooming mitt or a damp cloth or sponge—and the thin skin over bone here is more easily cleaned than the rest of the coat, so no heavy combing is needed. One tip to remember: bots, about which we'll hear more later on, accumulate on the lower legs (and I've seen bot eggs halfway up at least two horses' bellies) and are a real problem in most areas of the country. These parasites are picked up in the horse's mouth and travel through its system. Some people use special bot knives to rid the horse of the yellow-colored eggs, while others use a safety razor. You can get rid of many of them by simply using water at about 104 degrees—tepid to quite warm—to wash the horse's legs. The warm water causes the eggs to hatch out outside the horse and the parasites quickly die.

Mane and tail combs are usually fairly wide toothed and may be plastic or aluminum. Aluminum is probably a better bet, as I've pulled a couple of plastic combs completely out of shape in badly snarled manes and tails. This tool is used to help remove tangles and snarls and burrs from mane, tail, and forelock. It is not simply dragged down through the mane or tail, unless you want a very skittish horse on your hands. If a tangle is particularly bad, put one hand close to the base of the hair, and use

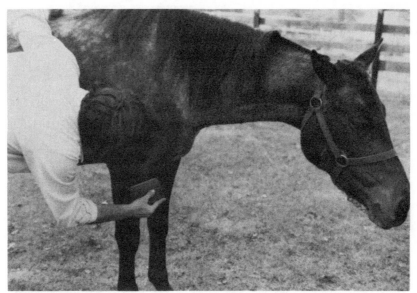

Fig. 82. Farnam Companies makes this block, which does an amazing job of removing grit, dust, and loose hair, while also getting off a good percentage of bot eggs.

the comb in the other, taking short strokes and keeping hold of the base of the hair to keep from yanking it out. Do the same at the tail.

Tail and mane trimming to keep a horse neat is sometimes a good idea, but in no case should the tail be trimmed to hang above the hocks. That tail serves as a built-in fly-swatter and can't reach all the places needed if it's trimmed too short. Manes can be trimmed in any number of ways, depending on your desires and the customs in your area. A roached mane, one that has been clipped to not much over an inch in length, is useful when riding in burr country for there's less hair for those blasted things to catch onto. This, too, is a good reason for not allowing a horse to keep a full and flowing tail.

For general use, there are three ways to trim a horse's mane and tail. Clippers can be used to get the length of both where you wish, and are almost essential if you want to roach a mane (in my area most people simply cut a bridle path, leave the forelock and the rest of the mane natural or near natural, and

Fig. 83. Teresa shows the correct technique for getting snarls out of a mane, gripping the hairs near the base and taking short strokes with the mane comb.

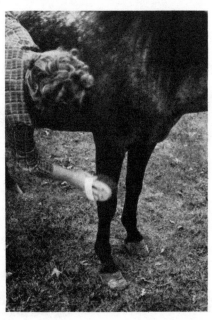

Fig. 84. Below-the-knees work is never done with anything stiffer than a good brush.

let it go). Better than clippers are trimming shears similar to those barbers use to thin out hair. Make sure any scissors or shears used around horses have blunt ends. The best method is pulling and thinning the mane and tail to the correct length and amount of hair.

To thin a mane or tail in this manner, you grasp half a dozen hairs you wish to remove and simply pull them out. Less is better, and more is impractical, for then the horse is going to become edgy as you'll be hurting him a bit. Do this slowly, bit by bit, so that you don't take out too many hairs and end up with a scraggly looking mane or tail.

When thinning a horse's tail, stand up as close to the rump as you can get and keep an eye on the forward movement of the animal's hind legs. If you get too many hairs at one pull, it may try and kick, and being able to see such a move coming and stepping to one side or the other is a handy defense. Staying in close to the rump is a defensive move in the sense that, if the horse does manage to kick you, the power of the kick is reduced by the short distance it travels. Any horse that kicks, for any reason, must be immediately disciplined. Don't wait five minutes to go and get your lunging whip. Do the job then and there, within a few seconds of the kick. Otherwise the punishment will simply confuse the animal and won't serve its intended purpose.

Breaking a horse of the kicking habit is often a fairly easy job. A slight tap just below the hocks with a lunging whip will, after two or three times, usually do the job. The idea is not to beat the animal to death, nor to relieve your own anger at being the target. You must want the horse to know, and remember, that every time it presents its rump to you, it must not even set up in kicking position.

WASHING YOUR HORSE

Washing and shampooing horses is often needed to remove fungi, as well as get rid of heavily caked sweat and mud. Horses used for show purposes are sometimes washed the day before the show and groomed out so thoroughly it is hard to believe

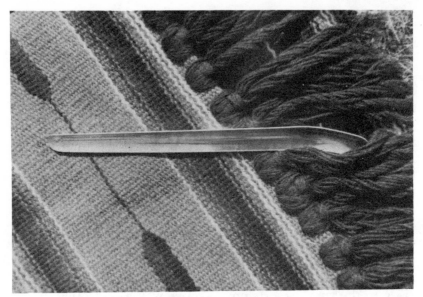

Fig. 85. A sweat scraper.

one animal could be so clean. Of course, common sense is a
large help when getting ready to wash any animal. First, the
weather is of great importance. Horses, like most animals, are
susceptible to disease. Getting them wet and allowing them to
stay that way on a cold windy day is a good way to bring on
problems. And just as most of us aren't all that happy with cold
showers, turning a cold water stream on a horse is usually just
asking for it to shy away. On the other hand, a hose full of
water that has been lying in the sun can be uncomfortably hot.

If cold water is to be used, it should be misted on the animal
so that the shock isn't great. Still, it's best to use lukewarm
water, even if that means attaching the hose to indoor taps. No
horse that's still hot from use should be washed with cold or
warm water. Cool the animal out first.

Horses can be washed with buckets and sponges as well as
hoses. Simply wet one side of the horse well and work the
shampoo from a second bucket into a good lather. It's more or
less up to you, but I like to start with the feet and move up the

horse so that the legs remain wet from the run-off. If a bucket is used, and the horse is done one side at a time, use another bucket of water to give a rough rinse to the coat before moving on to the other side. After doing the final side, shampoo the mane and tail, and use as many buckets of water as necessary to get all the shampoo out of the coat.

It is always best to use a shampoo specially made for horses, as these are formulated to do the least damage to the coat and will provide the best luster once the animal is dried.

Drying begins with the sweat scraper, which is used to squee-gee off excess water. Then use a couple of soft towels to finish drying, roughing up the coat in the process. A final rubdown with a soft brush, and your hand, should give the coat a really fine gleam.

All sorts of gadgets are made to attach to the end of a hose and serve as scrub brushes while water is flowing. Many of these are quite good and you may wish to experiment with one or two.

If your horse has been washed, dried, and is to be turned out to pasture, chilly days that are not really cold may have you wanting to put a light blanket on its back. My feeling is, unless a show is coming up, rather than blanketing such an animal, I would not shampoo it at all, using dry grooming methods instead. If the coat seems too oily and sweaty for dry grooming to help, use one of the dry shampoos. These are not as efficient as a good washing, but will be much less likely to cause health problems. If no dry shampoos are available, you can go to a local sawmill or lumberyard and pick up a couple of gallons of hardwood sawdust. Rub this into the coat, and then groom it out. It will carry an awful lot of dirt with it, and is about as cheap a coat cleaner as you can get. (Hardwood sawdust is best because softwoods, such as pine, contain gummy resins that serve to mess up the coat worse than at the outset.)

Incidentally, if your horse is one of the many that likes a good roll in the dust after a ride, let him get the rolling over with before you start grooming. The view of a freshly groomed horse rolling in dust or pasture is not one to fill the person who has just worked for an hour or two with great joy.

SHOW GROOMING

Show grooming involves a few more steps than does basic grooming, but is really not much harder. The basics are the same as the ones we've already covered, but such things as trimming the mane and tail are of greater importance—and there are a couple of additional steps that greatly aid your chances of winning.

First, the mane and tail are trimmed to the style you decide, usually at least partly specified by the rule book of the particular breed association. The American Horse Show Association also puts out a rule book covering various breeds, with its rule book being used in sanctioned shows by many breed associations. Generally, trimming the tail to fall at or just below the hocks will meet most requirements.

The mane, though, can be trimmed in different ways so that you're able to accentuate good points along the horse's neck, or at least partly cover up bad points. As an example, roaching the mane on a thin-necked horse will make the neck look a bit thicker, while the thick-necked horse is best served by having the mane left as long and full as possible. A mane that has a part and thus hangs on both sides of the horse's neck is not good in shows, so you may wish to place the entire mane to one side and then tie wet towels over it so that it will be more easily kept in place.

Show-groomed horses will also have the hairs inside their ears clipped, while general-use horses will not. The clipping here is purely for cosmetic purposes, but you've little chance of getting a ribbon if it isn't done. The hairs should not be clipped on a horse not being shown, as they serve to protect the ears when small flies start darting around the animal's head.

Show horses will also have the under-jaw hairs trimmed off; these hairs are often of greater length than other facial hair and can be clipped, though many people burn them off with a candle. If you decide to try this process, use extreme care and make sure the horse is securely cross tied.

To add a final bloom—or look of bloom—to your show horse's coat, the use of a conditioner is almost essential. In

Fig. 86. A cleaning block, and two currycombs. The metal currycomb requires more care and less pressure.

actuality, no conditioner can do much for the coat of a horse that is in bad shape. The natural oils and basic muscular shape and condition brought on by good routine care of the coat, proper nutrition, and exercise are all essential to a good-looking, glossy coat. Today, though, so many competitors add to this natural sheen with commercially available products that anyone in the show ring not using them is at a distinct disadvantage. You may well have to consider your horse's preferences when applying a coat conditioner. Some horses simply cannot abide the hissing sound of the many sprays on the market, and you may be forced to spill the conditioner on a cloth and rub it in.

When coat conditioners are applied, they need to be rubbed in well, in the direction of the natural lie of your horse's hair. For best results, use a fairly heavy application the afternoon of the day before an event, and then use a lightly coated rag to touch your horse up shortly before the show. Coat conditioners are always applied after a thorough grooming and shampooing.

Use a soft bristled brush after rubbing in the last application of coat conditioner for best possible results. This really brings out a shine.

CLIPPING

Once winter starts to approach, horses begin to grow their shaggy coats in preparation for the cold. For most purposes, we can just allow this coat to grow, especially if the horse is maintained on pasture and not stabled during cold weather. In fact, for the outdoor horse, clipping is definitely not a good idea, just as it isn't a good idea for us to stand outside in chill wind blasts with nothing more than our bare skin to cover us.

Part of the idea of spending a great deal of time grooming and fussing over our horses is to get them used to our presence, and to make them feel secure around us, so that clipping a horse and then leaving it to nearly freeze just doesn't fit in. Any pastured horse that has been clipped must be blanketed with a good-quality blanket. Unclipped horses provided a reasonable amount of shelter from high winds tend to do very well with no further care, with the possible exception of those areas that are almost ridiculously cold and icy.

To clip a horse, you can use either hand or electric clippers. Today, I would generally advise that for extensive clipping electric clippers save time and energy, though they can tend to make some horses very skittish because of the constant buzzing noise and the heating up of the cutting head. For simple mane roaching, a pair of good, sharp hand clippers is sufficient.

If you do intend to show your horse clipped, get a good pair of clippers and at least three sets of body hair blades for it. Blades dull as you cut, and a coat trimmed with dull clipper blades probably looks worse, from a judge's standpoint, than does a shaggy winter coat.

Start the clipping process with a routine grooming and shampoo to remove all dirt and most of the heavy oil from your horse's coat. Both of these substances will dull clipper blades, or clog them, and clipping a dirty horse will probably force you to have a dozen sets of blades on hand.

Pull the mane and tail first, so that you can see if there will be a need for further trimming in those areas. Roach the mane, or cut the bridle path. The forelock is left long no matter how the mane is trimmed, and usually a lock is left at the base of the mane, so that it can be gripped for mounting.

Start at the front of the near side of your horse and move the clippers smoothly down the coat. If your horse tends to shy, placing a ball of cotton in each ear may help cut down on that. Do both sides of the body and the belly first; many people prefer to leave the hair under the saddle long.

Clipping is done against the growth of the hair, and you'll need to spend some time investigating the whorls and swirls in the hair patterns over different body areas of your horse. Some of these hair patterns seem to go off in half a dozen different directions, and if you intend to do a good job of clipping, you will pay attention to them. Clipper heads are kept flat so you don't gouge the horse, but, in any case, cross tie the horse before starting. If muscles make an indentation, simply pull the skin flat, using your free hand, before going over the area.

Clipping the bony parts of your horse, around the face and legs, for instance, requires a great deal of care to prevent gouging and, because the hair coat is thinner and the skin lies so close over the bone, cuts in the skin.

The insides of the forelegs are most easily clipped from the opposite side, and the insides of the upper forelegs are best done with the foot resting on a support at least eighteen inches off the ground. This flexes the foreleg and fills out a lot of depressions, thus making trimming easier and giving a smoother clip.

When you're clipping the face be especially careful not to let the clippers touch the eyes. Your best bet is simply to cover the eye with your thumb while clipping, thus cutting out any chance of damage there. The odds are excellent that by the time you get to the head, the horse, no matter how willing to stand for clipping, is going to be a bit tired of the process and may start to move its head around a bit. Such conditions can cause a lot of chances at gouging, so great care is needed.

Once your clip is completed, wash and dry your horse again.

This does two things. First, it removes any loose hairs left in the coat by the clippers. Second, it will fluff the coat up nicely so you'll be able to tell if you've missed any areas. If you miss areas, trim them immediately after the horse is dry. If you wait a day, the rest of the coat will have grown some, giving you a strange-looking path on the trimmed area. Brush your horse down and apply a coat conditioner.

As you work at clipping, keep a check on the clipper head. First, look for dulling blades. It's easy to see when the blades become too dull to use as they start to leave tracks in the coat. Second, check the temperature of the cutting head. If it feels uncomfortably hot to you, your horse isn't going to like it either. You have the choice of having an extra set of clippers on hand or stopping and waiting for the head to cool down to a comfortable level.

If you keep a blanket on your clipped horse, it will serve almost as a daily grooming after clipping. The constant friction from the horse moving inside the blanket will keep the coat shiny, and the heat will cut back on new winter coat growth.

Some horses look better after clipping than do others. Generally, a gray horse shows less of a sheen than do most darker colors, but because of this the coat tends to look good more easily when clipped. If you have a buckskin, the horse will not change colors at all, but lighter-colored bays tend to come up sort of mouse colored after clipping and may take several days to regain their more natural coloring. Sorrels tend to lighten up in color.

Expect your first clipping job to take a fairly long time. Even those who are experts expect to spend over two hours with the clippers, so a first-timer is likely to run up over three hours and might hit four if the animal is fractious.

Clipping is a job for those showing in cold weather. Don't clip a summer coat unless you want a poor clip job and wish to wait almost an entire year for a new and good coat to come back. And don't turn a freshly clipped horse out if the weather warms up. The coat can sunburn and take some time to come back to normal.

Generally, grooming a horse may extend from nothing more than wiping off matted sweat and hair that would fall under the saddle area to complete show readiness. Most of us fall somewhere between these two extremes, though if you're closer to the first I hope for your horse's sake you also add in the daily hoof checks. Grooming provides a good method of getting to know any horse better, cuts down on possible boredom of stabled horses, and should quickly increase the knowledge you have of handling horses. A horse that is handled and ridden often is almost always an easier to handle and ride horse than one that is simply ignored. The psychology of having attention paid provides you with a great opportunity to get closer to your steed in understanding and, often, in your own feelings.

USING INSECTICIDES

Chemical parasite control is a fact of life for the modern horseman, and there are a variety of external parasites that force the spraying, rubbing on, leaving of baits, and other measures to prevent anything from extreme irritation to disease in your horse. While, in general, external parasites are the cause of what could be classified as a condition where the hair and skin are in rough shape and the overall vitality is lowered, these insects also are responsible for carrying some of the nastiest equine (and human) diseases known.

The basic control is one of good sanitation, with manure being removed and composted away from the barn or stable area, basic good-grooming procedures, and not allowing too many horses to live in too small an area. From this point, we must usually move on to some sort of chemical-control program.

The parasites themselves come in a wide variety of forms, as do all types of insect life. The blowfly lays eggs—maggots—in wounds from whence they spread all over the body, using the skin surface as feed. Weakness and fever soon follow.

Biting flies and mosquitoes of many types are of greatest trouble in warm weather, and can carry several serious equine

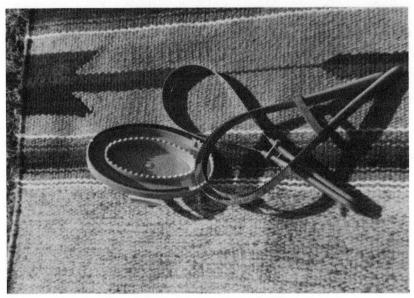

Fig. 87. All three of these tools are shedder/scrapers.

diseases as well as interfering with the development of young horses, and cause general malaise. Horse, deer, stable, and horn flies are the most usual.

Nonbiting flies such as the face fly and the house fly are also problems for horses and horsemen. Face flies cause an excessive flow of saliva and tears, while the house fly can transmit several diseases, human and equine, and may also carry stomach worms.

Lice of two types afflict horses. They are the horse-biting louse and the horse-sucking louse. Scabs may form over bites, the horse will show signs of intense irritation and will lose condition quickly, often spending a great deal of time scratching or rubbing against hard surfaces, and may also gnaw at its skin. While grooming, look for lice around the root of the tail, on the insides of the thighs, in the area of the fetlocks, and along your horse's neck and shoulders.

Mites cause irritation, itching, and a lot of scratching, after which the skin may crust over and become tough and wrinkled, with mange appearing at some point. When mange appears, you are required to report it to state or federal animal health authorities.

Ringworm is caused by a fungi, and the symptoms are round, scaly bald areas around the eyes, ears, on the sides of the neck, or at the root of the tail.

Screwworm symptoms are the loss of appetite and lowered vitality in general. The disease is caused by larva left by the screwworm fly. Most screwworm occurs in the South and Southwest, though recently the screwworm has been eradicated east of the Mississippi River.

Ticks of all kinds are found on horses, and again the signs will be lowered vitality and itching. Ticks may also spread several serious equine diseases.

As we've said, control of external parasites starts with good sanitation and grooming: grooming will also help you keep track of any infestations. Once that occurs, it is best to check with your local extension agent for the best insecticides available, including the types wiped or sprayed on horses, the types used for space spraying, and the bait types used around stables. Several broad-range insecticides are available, but some specific types may be required in places where, for instance, tick infestation is particularly heavy; obviously, when a horse is tick infested, the ticks must be removed and the areas disinfected, but the treatments for areas prone to their growth may include chemicals such as malathion, ronnel, and the pyrethrins. In each case, you should determine what application is needed and follow instructions carefully.

As an example of the complexity in using insecticides, the control of the psoroptic mange mite and sarcoptic mite require the use of any of three different chemicals, either as a spray or dip, with two treatments ten to fourteen days apart. These are federally approved, though you must still report the mites and the results, and federal inspectors will probably check out your methods, for you must also quarantine infested animals.

No matter what insecticide is required and recommended, and no matter who does the recommending, treat each one with care, for one thing they all have in common is the fact that they're poisons. Some horses will react badly to some common forms of spray or wipe-on insecticide, while others will be bothered little, if at all. Always try a new body contact insecticide on a small area of the horse first. If it causes hair loss or other problems, don't use it on that horse anymore. Sometimes simply reducing the concentration will help, too. Insecticides used as space sprays or baits must also be treated with care, and it is wise to wear some form of protective face mask when doing such spraying—and keep the animals out of the area being sprayed. Bait insecticides should be placed so that they cannot be reached by horses, other pets, and small children.

There are several electronic bug killers now on the market, and I regret to say I have no experience, and have met no one with such experience, of their use around horses. If they do work, they could be of great value in many stable areas.

Insect foggers using either electricity or propane to power the foggers are of some help in ridding outdoor areas of insects affected by pyrethrin-containing insecticides. The overall job they do is one of temporary control, though, and the effects are never long lasting.

In any case, whether fogging or spraying indoors or out, make sure you don't get the material on water supplies, feed supplies, feed mangers and bins, and other such areas. Animals shouldn't be returned to sprayed areas until these areas have had a chance to dry completely.

Insect control is a constant job around horses—or anywhere else. It is important, and needs a large part of your attention because of that importance. External parasites are not the only parasitic threat to your horse, but because the effects are most easily determined during grooming, they're included in this chapter instead of later on when internal parasites receive their share of attention.

5. MORE
SADDLE TIME

As your time mounted increases, so will your desire to add to your skills on horseback, especially if you're in an area where many people ride skillfully. You'll have been to shows and have seen the flashy sliding stops used in contests, and, often, in roping. You'll be eyeing some of the steeper hills and deeper valleys in your locale, wanting to go up or down to see what is there.

Much of the technique required for riding hilly terrain comes more or less naturally as you gain experience in the saddle, get to know your horse and its points of balance, and gain an eye for trail developments that may cause problems. The last point holds great importance for anyone wanting to ride broken country, for, as Tony Crilley told me recently, "When I first saw the aerial maps of the areas we were to cover in Arizona, I didn't think anyone could get through on foot, never mind on horseback!" Yet Tony spent years riding that country, and loved almost every minute of the time. Eyes for country can't be developed by a book, though. The only way to learn is to go out and ride. Ride with a more experienced companion if possible, but ride and ride often through broken country and you'll soon learn what to look for when one trail appears impassable. You'll learn to identify game trails, and discover which types of shale deposits are more likely to slide than others. Horsemanship in general requires experience, but riding rough country demands it, and no written word can even begin to do much more than tell you how to sit your saddle.

After that, it's up to you.

Position in the saddle varies with the rider, at least to some degree. Much depends on your build, your basic riding style, and what you expect to be doing. As an example, you can almost bet that a roper will use a stirrup an inch or two higher than will a rider using a cutting horse. The reasons are simple: the shorter stirrup makes it just that little bit easier for the roper to swing off the horse as the calf snubs up against the rope, while the cutting horse rider wants a secure, solid seat, deep down in the saddle for those times when his horse takes out after a steer at a 150-degree angle.

The basics are still followed, though. You ride erect, relaxed, keep your heels down, and stay alert for any moves your horse may make. Lower leg contact is essential so you're able to use leg cues with one or both legs. Pick up the reins so that you have contact with the horse's mouth when your hand is directly over the saddle horn; then, to get a slack rein, move your hand a few inches forward.

The hand is kept low, nearly on the horse's spine, so the animal's head will stay low. A low head is always desirable in a Western horse, for there is often a need for the horse to watch footing in rough country, or to watch stock being worked. High-headed horses may look showy as all get out, but they are best confined to arenas and areas where footing is always secure.

Watching a horse's ears helps keep a rider in tune with its mood and possible coming actions, even while mounted. When you mount, the ears will normally be turned back to you, though if the horse is really familiar with you they may not. One or both ears may flick forward as you break into a walk, but they should return to a central or rearward position immediately after your horse checks the trail. If you have no real problems, then you can expect to see one ear turned to you and one pointed on down the trail. As the horse becomes more used to your riding style, assuming, still, that nothing upsetting has occurred, both ears will probably point on down the trail.

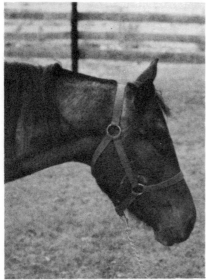

Fig. 88. As sleepy as she is, Patches still keeps her ears pointed toward the person holding her lead line.

Fig. 89. Someone has now walked behind Patches, so that her ears now point to the rear. Note they're not laid back, but only pointed, showing attentiveness, but not irritation.

Horses with laid-back ears are obviously not in a good mood, and mounting a strange horse with laid-back ears is an excellent method of finding out just how fast you can get in a saddle, and how well you can stick, once there. The ears can also focus on objects off to the sides, often long before the rider is aware of the presence of anything.

If you come upon a horse with its ears not pointed anywhere in particular, you can almost bet the horse is half asleep, or off in some sort of equine reverie. If this is the case, no matter how well you know the animal, speak softly to it while approaching so that it will know you're there and not be snapped back, startled and kicking, into the present.

As you ride ever rougher trails, trail footing becomes of great importance, and your seat on the horse can be either an aid or hindrance to your animal's ability to make it over or around obstacles. One essential to good riding technique in rough country is the ability to stay in one place in the saddle while the horse picks its way through. Moving around, sitting on one hip, tend to throw a horse a bit off balance, and at such times, the horse needs all the balance it can get.

There are times when you don't want to have your weight exactly in the middle of the saddle, but even then you shouldn't be wriggling around like a hooked eel. On steep uphill grades moving your shoulders forward a bit to place more of your weight over your horse's withers is a good idea, but hold the position until the horse clambers over the rim; don't go jogging forward and back. In the same way, on a very steep downhill you may wish to lean back a bit, placing some of your upper body weight over the cantle to aid in traction. Again, stay that way once you're there. In both cases, any such movement is dictated by your skills and by the terrain, but in no case should the movement be really extreme.

As time passes, you'll find yourself riding more tight patterns at higher and higher speeds, possibly in practice for contests such as barrel racing or pole bending, or more likely just because it feels good to get out and hammer the wind a bit. Because we've already covered changing leads, we'll go ahead and assume you're in the proper lead for each turn. You'll find as you ride that a certain amount of lean on your part may well add to your speed around the turn, may even make it possible for your horse to get a bit closer to the pole or barrel. But . . . you'll soon find that constantly leaning more and more, either to make up for the horse's angle of lean, in which case you'll be leaning away from the pole, or trying to lean into the turn to get a tighter turn, will only force your horse to compensate to balance your weight. Forcing the horse to feel for its balance will slow it down, and adds to your chances of taking a fall.

Again, then, the expert technique is to feel out the best

saddle position, get it quickly, and keep it. In almost all aspects of expert Western riding, the seat remains a balanced one, heels down, back straight, and the rider stays with the horse, neither ahead of, nor behind, its movements, though the top rider will be anticipating the next move of the horse so that the seat remains the same. The less expert rider will often be ahead of or behind the horse, and will fail to anticipate, allowing the animal's movement to throw him around in the saddle, forcing the horse, and the rider, to work that much harder to gain speed and keep its feet.

For trail riders, some different things need to be kept in mind when riding in company. Basically, they are points of consideration for others, and yourself, that make the ride more enjoyable and safer. As a beginning, good trail riders don't crowd the horse in front where the trail is not wide enough to ride other than single file. On wooded trails, keep the distance long enough to prevent a branch let go by a rider leading you to move back without slapping you or your horse in the face. If you have to pass another horse on the trail, keep your horse in check and don't slam by at a gallop. If you feel a need for a gallop while on a trail ride, get by the other horse at a just slightly increased pace, then, when clear, let your horse out for a run.

When doing something that requires a halt, whether it is taking pictures, adjusting a cinch, or watering your horse, get off the trail so that riders behind you can pass.

Of course, with only one or two riders other than yourself, some of these rules will be modified, but courtesy is a large part of expert horsemanship and is never out of place.

One trail rider's tip that can save some pain is more often seen among English-style riders: if your horse kicks, tie a piece of yarn or ribbon to its tail. This serves as a warning to any riders coming up behind you. Better yet, of course, is to break the horse of the kicking habit promptly, but sometimes, especially with a new horse, this isn't immediately possible, so a warning to others is in order.

Trail riding brings to mind another technique of riding: putting your horse in reverse. Backing can sometimes be the only way out of a tight corner on a bad trail, so the Western trail horse needs to back easily and calmly on command. For shows, the horse must back in a straight line, and for best control, the trail horse should do the same.

Most trained horses will already know how to back when you get them, so look for a horse that does the job properly. Backing should take place willingly, with head held low and with light and easy steps. While the head should be low, it shouldn't be tucked into the chest, nor should the horse rush back with its back down and legs asprawl. In nature, a horse seldom backs more than a step or two, so we have to work to get this movement (for training methods, see Anthony Amaral's *How To Train Your Horse*, Winchester Press, 1977) and keep the horse in practice. But because the movement over more than a few steps is not natural, your horse may quickly sour on backing if it is practiced too often. Once the horse is trained to back, keep any practice to just a few minutes each time, a couple of times a week, and never stop the horse more than twice after the same number of steps. Stopping each time after, say, five steps is liable to set up a habit pattern, so the horse will refuse to back further than five steps at a time.

Learning to stay with a good Western horse during a fast, sliding stop is a part of expert horsemanship that all of us need to acquire as soon as possible. Then we can hope we never need the skill outside the practice ring or arena. A proper stop for shows includes the horse bringing his rump down, getting his rear feet under him, and, as the saying goes, "dying on the spot." The head will come up so the animal can keep its balance, but the front legs, too, will stay on the ground. The front legs, though, will carry little of the horse's weight in a proper stop, and this is a point where the rider determines the effect. You must give the horse time to get its hindquarters under its rump, to gather itself for the stop. Sometimes, as on sudden emergency stops on the trail, this won't be possible, but generally it is. By the same token, not giving the horse time to gather itself for a stop may mean a bouncing stop, with the forelegs taking much of the strain.

Stopping doesn't require a heavily hauled back rein if the

Fig. 90. Doug Meador brings his horse along at a good pace, giving the first cue for a stop.

horse is properly trained and hasn't been soured. Hauling back on the reins keeps the horse off balance, making it use the hindquarters for balance instead of the head and neck as it would in a correct stop. Again, use technique, not power.

When practicing sliding stops, use skid boots on your horse so that he doesn't end up with fetlock burns. Start with the boots and always use them when practicing, as this sort of stop uses a lot of the horse's resources and adding sore fetlocks to the other work will soon cause just about any horse to sour on stopping quickly. It is probably a good idea, during practice, to have the horse back a step or two or three about every third or fourth stop. Two reasons exist for this. The backing helps the

Fig. 91. Note the horse setting up, the rear feet in line and the hindquarters coming under the horse.

horse to collect himself after the stop, and, during a trail ride emergency stop, you may well slide right up on the edge of a precipice. Getting back from there quickly will help calm both you and the horse.

For best results in stopping, the rider stays with the horse, not ahead of or behind. A balanced and steady seat is used so the horse does most of the work of stopping without interference from the rider.

Crossing water is a basic trail-riding problem for many riders. Many horses don't like to cross water, while others will go on across with no trouble. Some tend to rush the crossing, which is a fine way for both horse and rider to get a good dousing, and possibly take a fall.

All horses react differently to water, and the reactions can

Fig. 92. Because the ground was hard—the slide was short and the rump a bit up in the air—this isn't a perfect show stop, but it will surely do as any other kind. You'll note that Doug had both splint boots and skid boots on the horse. We were unable to find any soft sand or loam for the sliding stops, so protection for the horse was essential.

easily vary over the course of a day. The horse that has never balked at crossing may refuse a stream because it runs more rapidly, thus more noisily, than other streams it has crossed. The horse that has always shied at water may trudge right on across—or it may bolt across. Generally, when a horse is getting ready to rush a stream, you can feel it bunching, gathering its muscles for the leap. It's your job to be prepared for this and best if you can control the horse before it hits the water and uncertain footing.

If the day is warm, you get in midstream, and your horse starts to balk and bunch up, you've arrived at a good time to put the spurs to the animal and get it out of there, for it is most likely getting prepared for a good roll in the shallows. As my wife, Caroline, found out some years ago, even the world's weariest plodder is likely to sit slap down in a stream sometimes. Caroline says that was about the only time that old horse showed any energy.

Water depth and speed of flow play parts in the technique needed to cross water. If the depth is up on the horse's barrel and stream speed is quite fast, you'll need to head a bit upstream to reach a trail directly opposite you on the other shore. If the water is deep enough to swim, hold on to the reins loosely (so the horse can keep its head up and stretch its neck) and slip out of the saddle, swimming beside the horse. Don't get in front of the horse unless you enjoy being rolled under and possibly trampled. For this reason, it's also not a good idea to lead a balky horse across water. It may well rush right on over you as you tug the lead.

Keep contact with the horse as you swim alongside, for you'll want to swing into the saddle as soon as the horse's feet touch bottom, for it's at this point that many horses will tend to rush up out of the water onto the bank.

Care of the horse is important, too. If you've been riding hard enough to work up a lather on your horse, don't put it into a cold stream until the horse has time to cool out quite a lot. While a warm horse may enjoy a cooling dip or splash through a stream, one that is hot is almost surely going to develop muscle cramps.

As you can see, expert riding demands more of the rider, as well as of the horse, but the essential premise is one of not interfering with your horse as he does his job, whatever that may be. Use leg cues (cuing with the right leg will move the horse *away* from that leg, or to the left, and vice versa) firmly, and with some horses use spurs, *but use them as they are meant to be used.* Spurs used for Western riding are *always* blunted and are never used as instruments of punishment. Spurs are nothing more than somewhat stronger cue indicators for horses that may be reluctant to work with leg pressure, thus need a smaller pressure point and a firmer cue to work. They are used in back of the cinch, not in front, and are pressed firmly, but gently, into the cue area, not slammed in with toes pointed far out.

Aids such as spurs and bats, or whips, are auxiliaries to the basic reins and leg cues and need the same development of lightness as do the reins. Such aids have to cause discomfort if they're to be of any use at all, but must also stop short of causing real pain. The horse is intended to move away from the nudging discomfort of your leg, or your spur, but jabbing the animal to the point of real pain is likely to cause it to leap away in terror. Once you've got a horse terrorized, a great deal of work may well be necessary to make it a workable animal once more. So develop lightness in using the aids, though maintain the firmness, too.

Using an aid too lightly is like not having the aid, so firmness is also essential to good control of your horse. Without firmness, you have no control, so for that reason a bit, no matter how light your hands, must cause some discomfort, as must spurs. The less the discomfort, the better for both the rider and horse, for constantly inflicting pain on an animal is not at all pleasant. The good horseman wants a pleasant working relationship with the horse, but again the key word is working. You must be master and the horse your controlled subject, and all control must be done as lightly as possible, but with a firmness that will not allow the much larger and stronger horse to take advantage of you.

Expert horsemanship begins with the correct use of aids, extends through greater and greater control of the animal, and moves into the realm of anticipation. No matter the maneuver, whether a rollback, stop, change of lead, spin, pivot, or flat-out gallop, you'll be with your horse physically and just a bit ahead mentally, knowing and being ready for what's coming. When that time comes, you've put it all together and become a fine rider.

To do this requires daily practice, for the basic patterns used with the Western horse are learned skills for both horse and rider. Once your seat and hands are perfected, and you've learned to leg cue correctly, you can begin to work with the varying patterns.

Rollbacks are one place to begin learning the maneuvers needed in various riding conditions. In essence, you'll probably

Fig. 93. As the rollback starts, note the hocks under the horse. Doug is using a fence here, for the best way to train a horse to rollback is to turn him into a fence about six feet away (Doug's closer, but he's expert).

be training your horse to do the rollback at the same time you're learning to ride it yourself, for if you started extensive riding while reading this book, and not before, the horse, if trained to rollback, will probably have had enough time to at least partially forget the moves needed.

A rollback is not a tight turn in a circle. It is, as the name implies, a rollback over the hocks in which the horse comes to a stop, rolls back 180 degrees over its hocks, and takes off in the new direction. The rollback can be executed to the right or left, with the horse coming out of the right rollback on the right lead, and on the left lead from the left rollback. There is a moment of dwell as you stop, and then the horse is whirled into the rollback and jumped out, in the direction you prefer, using the correct leg and rein cues. Do the rollback in clearly defined stages, at first, working for precision and control. The leads

Fig. 94. The rollback continues.

will almost automatically be correct if you allow the horse time to gather itself. As your rollbacks become more precise, you can speed up the actual turn over the hocks, cutting down on that instant of dwell until it barely exists.

Your precision is helped by the pause after the stop, for one thing that quickly ruins any shot at a good rollback is reining the horse into the rollback before the stop is completed. All kinds of messes result, including crossed up feet, coming out on the wrong lead, and so on.

From rollbacks, you now make one more step and start working your horse in spins, or 360-degree turns. On the halfway mark of that step is the pivot, a sort of small, standing quarter turn to the right or left. To pivot, the horse must be settled, with its hind feet together, using the left front foot to push off for a right pivot and reversing that for a pivot to the left. The leg cue is made, for a left pivot, on the right side of

Fig. 95. Coming out of the rollback.

the horse and the rein hand should move back a bit to make good, light mouth contact then, in the direction of the pivot. The forelegs will rise from the ground and the horse will turn on its hindquarters and rear feet. You can start an untrained horse doing partial pivots until it gets the idea.

From the pivot to the spin is now simply a matter of adding the two together. The stop and rollback change your direction 180 degrees, and then you pivot to finish the 360-degree turn.

With both pivots and rollbacks, and the other more advanced exercises here, it is imperative that you don't work the horse too long. All of these maneuvers work a horse pretty hard, physically and mentally, so a few minutes work each day is plenty.

Once your horse stops well, rolls back, pivots, and spins well, don't overwork him. These are the basic reining-pattern requirements for horse shows, and top-reining horses are worked

Fig. 96. About to do another rollback—note that Doug is allowing his horse time to get set up.

only enough to keep them in trim and going well. If the horse stops going well, during or after training, work at something else. Take a well-varied trail ride. Find a couple of calves you can work at cutting (check with the owner first!). Do anything but the reining work for a few days, and then try your horse again to see how it's going. If the horse isn't completely soured on reining, all should now be well.

Now that you're working with the five basics, and can handle your horse at all gaits from a walk to a lope to a trot to a canter to a gallop, you will continue until you are truly an expert horseman, if you keep a few things about training yourself and your horse in mind.

Be patient. Patience is essential to horse training, of course, and is too often forgotten in the heat of wanting to get things done, but cannot ever be forgotten when applied to the horse-

Fig. 97. Spins start here . . .

man. Becoming a good rider and a good horseman isn't an overnight process, so have a bit of patience with your own development too.

Be satisfied with small steps and an easy pace or the horse will go sour on you, stopping any progress and often backing off and seeming to forget things already well learned. Take it easy, and don't overtrain any horse. Back off and work on another phase, or just go for a ride, instead of overtraining.

Don't practice in the same spot too often. You may get a few surprises if you keep your horse stopping at the same point each day for a week. Gallop by the next day and you may well be grabbing leather to stay on as the horse sets up and skids to a halt! Don't let the horse set up a pattern in its mind.

Keep rein pressure light! This is essential. Never, even as a beginning rider, use the reins to balance yourself. If you feel as

Fig. 98. . . . and continue here . . .

if you're falling off, grab the horn, but don't saw or jerk on the reins.

Keep other cue pressures as light as you can. Some horses work more easily to cues than do others, of course, but some are hard to work just because, for a period of time, someone used more cue pressure on spurs or legs than was really needed.

Teach your horse, and yourself, in stages. No subject as complex as riding a horse can be learned all at once, so start simple and stay simple with your steps, making sure that both you and your horse master each stage before presenting yourselves with the next challenge. Wait a day or two after mastering one phase before moving on to the next.

Follow general horsemanship rules as to care and conditioning of your horse, for you're asking it to respond like an athlete

Fig. 99. . . . and keep going.

in many of these maneuvers, so you should warm up, condition, and train it to shape up like an athlete or not ask as much from it.

Keep a particularly careful check on the rear fetlocks, even when using skid boots, during stopping, rollback, and spin practice, and keep a close eye on the hooves, making sure the trim is correct and the shoes fit properly.

Make sure the saddle, bridle, blanket, pads, girth, and all other gear fit the horse and your needs and are in good repair and as comfortable as possible.

The fit of tack to the rider and horse begins with the purchase, but too often the purchaser knows little or nothing of the intended purposes of different kinds of gear. For that reason, the next chapter will cover different style Western saddles, bridles, bits, chaps, and so forth.

6. TACK
AND CLOTHING

Any saddle is a fairly complex combination of metal, leather, wood, nails, screws, and odds and ends, but the Western, or stock, saddle is even more complex than most. Because riding in some form or another has been with us a bit over 4,000 years, and has changed a great deal, the saddle and other tack items we know today have had a long period of evolution—with our modern stock saddle owing a great deal to the saddles of the Spaniards back in the 1600s.

The saddle of the conquering Spaniards soon became a stock saddle for the use of cattlemen who followed the conquistadores. Because a lot of riding over long periods of time was essential to handling stock, a deep and comfortable seat was desirable. Other developments came into being as required over the years. The tapadera was placed over the stirrup to keep branches away in heavy brush country, and the saddle horn came into use so that riders could rope a hard-to-handle cow or steer.

As more time passed, different tree styles evolved to handle different jobs. A look at the tree of a roping saddle and one from a cutting saddle will show great differences. The roping saddle will have a fairly slick fork, so that dismounting is a bit easier once the steer is roped and down. The cutting-saddle tree will have a wider, undercut swell fork so that the rider has more support as his horse makes rapid changes of direction.

THE
SPANISH
WAR
SADDLE

16th Century

Fig. 100. Spanish war saddle, circa 1500. A very deep seat and wraparound cantle along with center-fire rigging dominated in this era. Credit: Tex Tan Western Leather Co.

SANTA FE
SADDLE
1800

Fig. 101. By 1800 styles had changed quite a bit, but the basics were similar. The horn was more developed, and the fork not as swept back, while the cantle had shrunk. The single rigging had moved forward to about the same spot as today's ¾ rigging. Credit: Tex Tan Western Leather Co.

TEXAS
TRAIL
SADDLE
1870

Fig. 102. Most directly related to the modern saddle is the Texas Trail saddle used in the 1870s. For the first time, some attention was paid to getting the bars to fit the horse and a rear rigging strap was added. Credit: Tex Tan Western Leather Co.

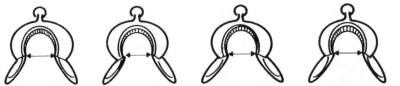

Regular 5½" Semi-Quarter Horse 6" Quarter Horse 6½" Arabian 6¾"
Fig. 103. Different bar styles for different horses. Credit: Tex Tan Western Leather Co.

Not only do the trees vary to suit the rider's purposes, but they vary to fit different horses. The shorter-backed Arabian will be exceptionally uncomfortable in a saddle built to fit a Quarter Horse, while the high-withered Thoroughbred will soon become sore under a saddle designed for the far broader back of the stock horse. For that reason, the saddle tree is of great importance when you select a saddle. It is the base for all that comes after and without a good, well-designed tree, no saddle is worth setting on a horse's back.

Today, stock saddles come with trees of three different materials, and most saddlemakers offer a representative sampling in their lines. Cheaper saddles will be of wood sprayed with fiberglass resin for reinforcement, while plastic trees (Ralide) are popular in some middle price ranges. The basic, working stock saddle, though, offers a wood tree, usually pine, covered with rawhide. Trade names, such as bullhide, are used to denote saddles with trees meant to withstand extremely heavy stresses. These trees are covered either with heavier rawhide or with two layers of rawhide.

The tree has several parts, all of which are designed for specific purposes. The bars of the saddle tree distribute a rider's weight over the back of the horse and are designed with five basic configurations to fit most horse breeds. Arabian bars are shorter, usually by three-quarters to one inch, than any other. Quarter Horse and full Quarter Horse trees have a wide spread at the gullet, often as much as seven inches, while a Regular tree offers about 5¾ inches at the gullet (an Arabian tree may be as wide as 6½ inches, though most are probably closer to 6¼ inches).

It's at the point of selecting bar types that some trouble may arise if you plan to ride many horses of different types. My roughout roper has full Quarter Horse bars, and is not good at all on Thoroughbreds, though it serves admirably for most of my riding purposes (these days I seem to spend a lot of time on Appaloosas). It is worthless on Arabians. For riding such horses, I either have to borrow a saddle or not ride, unless I have several extra pads (and the saddle still can't be used on Arabians). The extra pads, though, present another problem, as too much padding under a saddle tends to allow the saddle to slip on the horse's back.

So a saddle to fit the horse type you plan to ride is needed, but you may find you'll do as well with either semi-Quarter Horse bars (six-inch-wide gullet) or a Regular tree. The Regular tree will fit most horses fairly well, but is of little use for the wide-backed old-style Quarter Horse, or for some other stock breeds with very broad backs.

At the front of the saddle tree are the swells. They join the bars, and are also called the fork of the tree. Forks come in three basic styles, with literally hundreds of variations. Essentially, there are full forks, undercut forks, and extreme-undercut forks, with the occasional slick fork slipping in to add another to the basic list. Fork width ranges from about eleven to fourteen inches today, with full forks running about eleven to thirteen inches, most undercuts at twelve to thirteen, and extreme undercuts twelve to fourteen. Slick forks may be a bit narrower, but not too many people actually care for a slick fork saddle today.

Over the years, fork design has changed a lot in some ways, but generally seems to work its way back to some variation of the basic three. Undercut and extreme-undercut swells are most useful for cutting work and riding in rough terrain, while the full swell makes a fine base for a roping saddle.

Any Western working saddle is, or should be, built to take the strain of roping. The horn is the tie-off or dallying post for the rope and must be built to take repeated strains. As well as working as a snubbing post for roping, the saddle horn is the supreme handle when you find yourself on top of a horse that

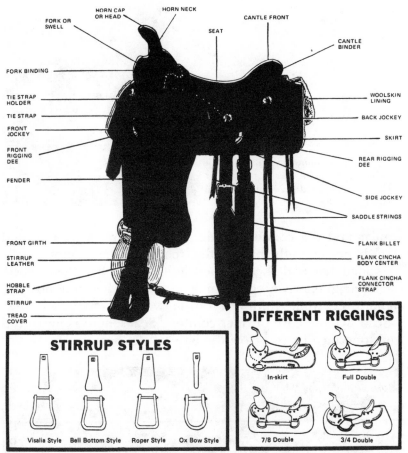

Fig. 104. The parts of a modern saddle, along with the different stirrup styles and rigging styles.

decides on what is known as instant rodeo. They're also not bad for wrapping a leg around while you try to roll a cigarette in imitation of a movie cowboy; you can hook the leg and watch your tobacco fly into the wind. Various horn shapes are found, but the good saddle will have a horn of cast brass or iron attached to the fork with screws and bolts.

Having assembled this much of a saddle, we're still missing two major portions of the tree, the cantle and the seat. The cantle is the back of the seat and comes in two basic styles, the

Fig. 105. The author's saddle. As a not so incidental point, this is the proper way to stand a saddle when no saddle rack is available.

regular and the comfort cantle. Regular cantles have a mild arch shape across the back of the tree, while the comfort cantle is shaped flat and then dipped away from the rider's back. Cantle heights may range from two to five inches, but most are about three, while width varies from twelve to fourteen inches.

Seats are the base of rider comfort. Seat length is measured from one inch or so below the base of the horn to the center

Fig. 106. In skirt rigging.

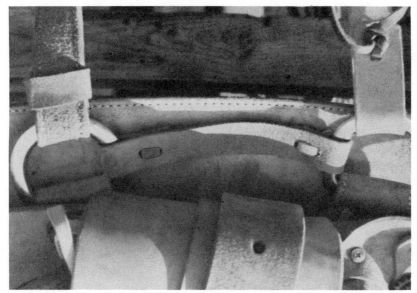

Fig. 107. Connected full-double rigging.

Fig. 108. Note how my saddle has no fork swell back. This roping model makes for ease in dismounting.

Fig. 109. A cutting saddle has more security. The rubber wrapped around the horn is cut from an inner tube and protects the horn covering during roping (roping is done from cutting saddles too).

top edge of the cantle. Seat sizes, for adult saddles, will vary from about thirteen to sixteen inches in length (on the tree, with no covering). The seat length should be proportioned to rider size, but build as well as overall height will have an effect on seat size, as will the design of the forks. For example, a seat of 15½ inches is my need on a padded seat saddle with a regular fork, and that's what I'm using now. If I used an undercut swell, I could shrink that seat size by about half an inch and be just as comfortable.

Rider preference must also be considered in selecting a seat size. Some people simply prefer a snugly fitted seat, while others like more room. It's a good idea to remember, though, that if you make a mistake in selecting seat size, you'll be a lot more comfortable if the seat's a bit too long rather than if it's a bit too short. The chart below provides a starting point for the person with an average build and is intended to provide seat sizes for saddles with padded seats (very few unpadded seat saddles are made today). If you do select a saddle with an unpadded seat, substract half an inch from the chart to get a starting measurement. In all cases, I would definitely suggest that you ride saddles of several sizes, if at all possible, before investing in your own.

SEAT MEASUREMENTS

Height/ Weight	Full Forks	Undercut Forks	Extreme Undercut Forks
5' to 5'5" 100 to 125 lbs.	14½"	14"	13" or 13½"
5'5" to 5'7" 115 to 140 lbs.	15"	14½"	13½"
5'7" to 5'10" 140 to 165 lbs.	15"	14½"	14"
5'10" to 6' 165 to 185 lbs.	15½"	14½-15"	14½"
6' to 6'2" 180 to 200 lbs.	16"	15½"	15"

And now, to go against my own recommendations, I'll tell you about my saddle. It has full swells, and the seat measures 15½ inches. I'm 6'2" and weigh just about 200 pounds most of the time these days. My legs are fairly long (I wear a thirty-four-inch inseam). My seat then is half an inch to an inch too short, supposedly. But there's sufficient room for me, and I find the saddle very comfortable, particularly since I moved from a fifteen-inch seat on a full swell saddle to this one. Again, personal preference plays a large part in selecting a saddle, and not just on the carving and fancy work (of which, mine has none).

The rawhide that covers the tree of a saddle is applied wet and allowed to dry on the tree, where it shrinks and becomes hard and very tough. Double, or heavier rawhide, coverings can be found on many heavy-duty saddles, but are not really essential unless you are a roping contestant. On wood trees with fiberglass coverings, the tree may first be covered with canvas before the resin is sprayed on, or the resin may be mixed with chopped glass fibers. No such saddle is suitable for anything other than pleasure riding of the mildest sort.

Ralide trees are injection molded in one piece, and are quite strong, carrying the same five-year guarantee as do well-made rawhide-covered tree saddles. Weight and price are generally a bit lower than comparable saddles with wood trees.

The seat on a wood tree is a built-up unit consisting of several layers, known as groundwork, on which the foam seat padding is added, after which the covering is stitched on.

Good-quality Western saddles are expensive even when not very fancy, and a large part of the reason is the cost of the leather. According to saddlemakers, a complete hide is necessary to build a good saddle.

Some checks are needed when buying either a used or new saddle to see what shape the leather is in. First, check for obvious scars, scrapes, and cuts, both on the exterior of the leather and the underside. Then flex the various parts of the saddle. No checking or cracks should appear in the leather, nor should any neatsfoot oil ooze out under such bending. On the flesh (rough) side of the leather, look to see that the fibers are tightly packed in any spots where strength may be required (stirrup leathers, skirts, etc.).

Rigging is mounted in several ways, and there are variations in the position of the front cinch that can affect your riding style in certain cases. Saddle rigging is made up of many parts, from latigos to cinch to dees, rings, and other parts. The rigging can be attached to the skirts, usually built in between two layers, or it may be attached to the tree. Rigging attached to the tree is considered the strongest, but some respected makers have worked for years with plate rigging without having a single one pull loose in the most extreme use.

Check the rigging rings first. They should be stainless steel or cast brass. If they're welded steel, the saddle is not as good. Any rivets used must be solid copper. Saddles may be either double or single rigged, though few people today use the center fire, or single, rig. Double rigging comes in full double (mounted the closest to the front of the saddle), seven-eighths double, and three-quarters double. There is about one to one and a half inch difference in mounting position in these different rigging positions, and in all cases the rear rigging is mounted in the same place. Some saddles offer a set-in plate that allows the use of any of the three positions.

Right now, my saddle is a double rig, full. At some future date, assuming continued income and a bit less inflation, I would like to have a seven-eighths or three-quarters double rig for use in steeper country, but the full double serves most purposes very well. The seven-eighths double is generally considered a bit more secure when you're on steep terrain (since it's a bit further back, you can use a slightly wider cinch without pinching your horse).

Saddle styles, types, and decorations range so widely that there is one for just about any personal preference. If you can't find exactly what you want, take a quick look through the offerings of some smaller custom saddlemakers, but expect to spend several hundred dollars more. A good saddle is in no way cheap to buy. Mine is about the lowest-priced rig in its strength class that I could locate, yet it cost just about $400 last year. The price has already jumped over that.

Expect to spend at least $300 for a good Western saddle, and probably more. What you spend will depend on your needs, for I paid for a heavy roping tree I don't really need in order to get a few other features I did. Custom saddles now seem to start at about $600, and prices are rising rapidly. If you spend that kind of money for a saddle, good care of the leather and other components is essential to make it last as long as possible. Later in this chapter, I'll cover taking care of saddles and other leather tack items.

Some show saddles are so expensive that almost daily care of the leather and silver would seem required. I went through a saddlery catalog a few weeks ago, from a company specializing in show saddles. It was easily possible to spend some $5,000 outfitting the horse and yourself—and you still wouldn't own a horse! Most Western shows specifically state that a good working outfit in good condition will not be marked down in favor of silver-mounted fancywork, but in practice that doesn't really happen too often, so most serious competitors feel they have to go for the expensive tack.

Once your saddle is selected, it's time to go and take a look at bridles. The basic Western bridle is of a simpler construction than is the English bridle, but that basic bridle has so many variations simplicity quickly runs off and hides in some dark

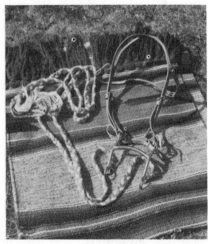

Fig. 110. Note my single-ear bridle style. I prefer this because of its simplicity.

corner. Each manufacturer has a preferred style, in addition to other styles, so that it isn't difficult at all to count about three dozen bridles from one maker. In many cases, the only real difference in such bridles will be the color or quality of construction.

Generally, a Western bridle will have a browband, headband, cheek pieces to which the bit is attached, and a throat-latch. The browband and its accompanying headband will sometimes be a single-piece unit with a section that fits only over one ear, while at other times it will fit over both ears, with separate holes for each ear.

From there, you move into quality of construction and decorative applications (some extremely heavily decorated bridles can cost upwards of $350!). Most Western bridles don't use nosebands, though many do come with them: many Western show classes prohibit nosebands (also called cavessons). The decoration you desire is up to you, but look for a bridle that is of doubled and stitched leather in preference to a single layer and of good-quality, medium-weight leather. Color and design should match your saddle for a good appearance, but that's not imperative. If your bridle is of good quality, it will last for many years.

Reins, like all other equipment, vary in style and purpose. So-called Texas-style reins are split. That is, each rein is separate. Historically, Texas cowboys dropped the reins to ground-tie their animals, so they naturally had to have reins that would split away and reach the ground. California styles are not split, but are joined in the center and have at their junction a quirtlike device called a romal. For a variety of reasons, Californio reins have never been very popular east of the Rocky Mountains, and the braided-leather bridles of that area have only slowly gained acceptance in other areas of the country.

Today, reins may be made of many materials instead of the old standby, leather. Leather, either braided, single strap, doubled and stitched, or in some other form, is still very popular and can be heavily decorated as well (prices of show reins get right up there with bridle prices, and sometimes even a bit higher). Nylon is popular in some areas, while in my own case I tend to prefer braided-mohair split reins. Whatever your choice, split or Californio, leather or fabric, look for good detailing and quality just as you should in all tack items. Prices for most simple reins aren't so high that it pays to economize much.

Halters are essentials for any horse owner, as are lead ropes. Leather may still be the most popular material for this device today, but a great many are now being sold in nylon and polypropelene rope styles, an improvement over older cotton rope styles. Nylon-web halters are also gaining in popularity. The reasons for the growth in popularity of synthetic material halters are many, one of them being that they cost about half what the cheapest leather halter costs. Another reason is that nylon will often outwear a leather halter since the sweat from a horse tends to deteriorate leather more quickly. In addition, the nylon halters require little, if any, care.

Lead ropes for halters are also available in many materials, actually in just about the same materials as are the halters. Halters may be plain or fancy, and if you decide to show your horse in a halter class it may well pay to get a lightly decorated halter and lead rope in leather for just that purpose. Otherwise the plainer styles serve as well, and usually longer, at much less expense.

Breasts collar are devices used to keep a saddle in place in rough going. Generally bought at the same time as a saddle, most breast collars will match the saddle in carving, color, and other decoration, but you will also find them of braided mohair that can be bought in colors to match your cinch.

Another note on halters is necessary. One of the prime aspects of horse safety is the adage about never leaving a halter on a pastured horse. It is too easy for the horse, scratching at flies, to hang a hoof in the halter, and too easy for the animal to get hung up on a low branch or other obstacle. In case your horse is a bit harder to catch and halter, and you feel a strong need to leave it haltered in pasture, I would recommend you purchase one of Farnam Company's safety halters. It has buckles and fasteners designed to break away under moderate pressure. These halters cost only a few dollars more than a comparable plain halter and are well worth every cent when you pasture your haltered horse.

Some horses are hard to approach when you're holding a halter and lead rope, or a bridle, yet are not at all difficult to get near when your hands are empty. In such cases, you could just consider using a piece of baling twine around the neck to lead the horse to the saddling point: a few horses will not come with this, but getting a long enough piece to toss a loop around the animal's nose as well as its neck will often serve with them. Make sure the twine is long enough to provide two or three feet of lead line. And a safety note: always lead the horse from one side or the other, and never, under *any* circumstances, wrap the lead rope around your hand. Keeping to one side prevents the horse, if startled, from running over you, while having the lead rope loose can prevent your hand getting caught if the horse bolts. Being dragged by a runaway horse is not a pleasant experience, and any horse that is terrorized or angry enough to bolt is going to be too strong for even the most powerful human to hold. Far better to let the animal run than to get yanked along with it.

BITS

At one time, horses were ridden without the control of much more than a rope tied around their necks. Bits came into being thousands of years ago and have been constantly refined and developed to a point where the multiplicity of design confuses even the experts. Most of us find one style or two styles or three styles, depending on the number of horses we ride, that work for us and tend to stay with them. The bit is the primary source of control for the horseman, and as such is of great importance to all of us. Selection should be made on the basis of several points, but foremost among the points is quality. On no basis is a cheap bit worthwhile. First, cheap bits rust quickly, which means they'll rapidly taste bad to the horse and need to be discarded. Second, cheap bits may well be nonsymmetrical, causing overcontrol on one side and undercontrol on the other. Third, cheap bits with movable cheekpieces often pinch a horse's mouth, causing poor, or no, control.

Considering the points of control in the horse's mouth may help explain why bitting properly is so important. First, the tongue is sensitive to pressure, and all mouth-held bits exert at least some pressure on the tongue. Second, the bars—that toothless space between the incisor and molar teeth—is a very sensitive area and a primary control spot. It is also one of the most easily messed up spots on a horse, for the sensitivity at the outset is so great that even a slight excess pressure over a period of time is enough to harden your horse's mouth. Bits exert pressure in two other areas. The lips are also very thinly covered with skin so the horse will react to pressure in that area. Snaffle bits, usually considered an English style, provide almost no pressure on the bars, but are effective in using the lips. Any such bit, with moveable portions, should have a bit guard to protect the lips from the pinching action of the bit.

The final bit control point is on the outside of the mouth, actually under the jaw. It is known as the curb groove and is the reason for curb chains and straps on Western bits. Here again, the skin covering is thin, thus very sensitive, and the selection of a curb strap or chain must be made with that in mind. In no instance should you use either a strap or chain that is less than half an inch wide, and all chains should be of the flat type to keep from inflicting pain.

Hackamores and bosals use slightly different pressure points to achieve the same results. Over the nose, skin lies very thin over sensitive nerves, and there is a point near the middle of the underjaw that is also very sensitive to pressure. The nose and the underjaw will receive pressure when a hackamore or bosal is used for control, and the nose may also receive some pressure if a curb bit is used with a nose strap.

With the number of pressure points available on a horse's head, you have a wide choice of options in selecting a bit or hackamore, and will be able to change from one to another should the horse respond badly to the first selection.

Curb bits of various kinds are the most popular among Western riders. The curb bit gives the rider a leverage advantage that varies according to the length of the shanks but is seldom less than two to one. In other words, applying twenty-five pounds of pressure at the reins causes a fifty-pound pressure on the sensitive areas—in this case, the curb bit will give pressure on the bars, the lips, and the poll (the top of the head where the top band of your headstall passes). It is for this reason we have so carefully emphasized the development of light hands for the horseman. A curb bit of even the mildest sort can cause a great deal of pain when the reins are yanked.

The bar that fits in the horse's mouth may be any of a hundred designs, with some almost straight across and others having a well-defined arch in the center (sometimes with a clicker in the arch, which is used to keep the horse from getting bored with the bit). Occasionally, you'll find a curb bit with loose cheekpieces, and sometimes there will even be a joint in the mouthpiece bar.

Some horsemen contend that the loose-jaw mouthpiece tends to create more moisture in the animal's mouth, which aids in keeping the mouth comfortable when the horse is bitted. The same is said for copper mouthpieces, and, in both cases, my experience has been that the contention is correct. My curb bits are stainless steel with copper mouthpieces. While I have no idea whether it is true, it is said that a copper mouthpiece will delay a mare's coming into estrus (heat), so these are seldom used by breeders.

When at all possible, I prefer a low to medium port mouthpiece. That is, a mouthpiece which conforms as much as possible to the shape of the bars and tongue. These are the least severe of the curb bits. Higher port styles decrease the pressure on the tongue, but increase the pressure on the bars. Lower port styles reverse the process. The thicker in diameter the curb bit mouthpiece is, the less extreme will be the pressure on either tongue or bars.

If you decide to select a high port mouthpiece with a cricket, or roller, do not expect the cricket to add to the severity of the bit, for its sole purpose is, as we said, to keep the horse from becoming bored with the bit. Some care in cricket design is needed. It must fill the entire area of the port. A partial cricket that's too small may well pinch the horse's tongue, which will certainly not aid control, nor make your horse any happier.

My familiarity with spade mouthpieces is limited to having watched them used and having read about them. Spade bits, and the related half-breed bits, are a complex subject and are seldom used in the East, for the training methods in working up to such a bit differ markedly. The port is extremely high in most of these bits, often going to four inches and sometimes more, which means the port is high enough to contact the top of the horse's mouth (most high port bits stop well short of two inches and are not intended to contact the roof of the mouth). A cricket is always used, and the mouthpiece is usually worked with copper to help keep moisture in the mouth. As I said before, spade bits are no more cruel than any other, if properly used, and often less cruel in the hands of an expert. Still, unless you are expert, and your horse is trained to work with a spade bit, it is probably better to leave them alone.

A good amount of weight is needed for a bit to be stable, and not rock back and forth in your horse's mouth, and generally steel bits are more desirable than those of lighter metals. In my case, I would far rather spend the extra money for a good, well-made stainless steel bit than for any plated or blued model. Simply put, that thirty-five-dollar stainless steel bit is likely to outlast a twelve-dollar plated model by about six to one.

At the same time, don't select a bit that has a lot of backsweep in the cheekpieces. Configuration here is also a point in control, and extreme backsweeps make it awkward for the horse to keep its head in working position.

In other words, try to avoid extremes. It is often necessary to experiment with bits to see which works best with a particular horse. Some animals are quite easily controlled with a bit that has no port at all, while others need the extra pressure on the bars provided by medium and high ports. Some horses, though, work better with more tongue pressure. In general, a fairly low or medium port and a thick mouthpiece will serve if the horse has a good mouth. Cheekpieces should be of moderate design, too, and I would totally avoid the severely swept back grazing bit.

Curb straps play an important role in controlling your horse and are available in wide variety. The mildest curb strap available is a plain, smooth leather strap, while a double-link flat chain is next. The single-link chain is the most severe. Curb chains, though, have a tendency to pull the longer hairs found in the curb groove—I usually trim any long hairs my horse may have around the curb groove, or, even better, use the milder curb strap when at all possible.

Again, you'll have to try and see. Fortunately curb straps of good quality are relatively cheap even today, so getting the proper one for your horse won't be too expensive.

HACKAMORES AND BOSALS

Three forms of hackamores are available today: the rawhide hackamore, the rawhide bosal, and the mechanical hackamore, or hackamore bit. There is some confusion over the difference between a hackamore and a bosal; they are more or less identical, except for the diameter of the nosepiece: a bosal is under half an inch in diameter, while a hackamore is thicker. The designation is important only in that the thinner diameter bosal is more severe, everything else being equal. Bosals and hackamores made of rawhide braided over rawhide cores are generally the least severe, while those braided over cable must be used with exceptional care to prevent soring the nose.

Mechanical hackamores offer rawhide braiding that works over the nose, in conjunction with cheekpieces and a curb

Fig. 111. This particular hackamore is a catgut model, wound around a rawhide core. It belongs to Jim Shands. Note the way the reins are tied on; out West much more complex tying methods are used.

strap. Leverage is a bit higher, but the hackamore bit can easily be decreased in severity by changing to a smoother noseband. For horses needing little severity, you can even get a soft sheepskin cover for the noseband (these can often be applied to regular hackamores, too).

The tighter the noseband, the more severe the hackamore, no matter the kind, so that a narrow hackamore with a rough rawhide noseband is very severe. Using a cable core for the noseband will add to severity because the springy cable will keep the noseband in constant contact with the sensitive portions of your horse's nose. Most people have no need for this degree of severity, and may well end up ruining the horse for hackamore work, or even peeling skin right off the nose.

OTHER TACK ITEMS

Outfitting the general-use horse is not complete with just the saddle, bridle, reins, bit, halter, and breast collar. A saddle blanket or pad is needed, and today we're running into some new designs that could change the entire process of saddling a horse, and caring for its back, in the near future.

The new saddle-pad developments are, I think, of special interest to us. First, the Poron Division of Rogers Corporation is now making the material for a closed cell-foam saddle pad. Second, Terry Raat of Crafters out in Colorado is making a type of pad/blanket called the Flow Form.

Both developments are a step in the right direction, since a horse with a sore back is not something any horseman wants. At first I thought the Poron pad sent to me would more likely cause problems than help them, but some extensive testing under a jumping saddle (the pad I was sent is English style) showed that it provided good padding, kept the horse a bit cooler, and stayed with the saddle, giving a nice, tight saddle fit with almost no saddle movement (one of the causes of soring). The circulation of air under the saddle was apparently better than with normal padding.

I've been unable to test the Flow Form saddle pad, but from material Terry Raat has sent me, I can only say it looks awfully good. Essentially, the pad is made of wool and has pockets to hold a material also used to fit ski boots. What happens is that the Flow Form material provides a form fit of the saddle to the horse's back, so that contact, and thus pressure, is spread evenly over the widest possible area.

Because every horse's back is shaped differently, the conventional saddle blanket, even with a hair pad, can't provide a perfect fit. The new developments should be welcomed by horses and horsemen everywhere. Cushioning the shock also involves matching the changing contours of a horse's back as it goes through different gaits: that back is never a totally constant shape, so the padding must move to conform.

Most of the new types of pads also get a tighter grip on your horse's back, so there is less saddle slippage, the rider thus has a better feel for the horse, and one more area of possible soring is eliminated, or cut back.

Saddle blankets and hair pads of good quality are still the all-time favorites, though many people are supplanting them with newer materials. In some cases, saddle blankets of good wool are still recommended for use under the new pads.

WESTERN CLOTHING

The sale of Western clothing in this country has surpassed the Western-style riding horse in growth for several years now. Jeans and snap-fastened shirts of Western cut are exceptionally popular in areas as diverse as the New Mexican desert and the streets of Manhattan. Of course, utility is a reason for the development of most of the features found in Western clothing, and that utility is not exactly essential to the world of concrete canyons. It simply isn't often, outside Madison Square Garden, that a person in New York City is likely to require the quick-opening feature of a snap-fastened shirt, for there simply aren't that many bulls or saddle horns on which a shirt can get hung up. Still, disco and drugstore cowboys surely outnumber riders of almost any kind, and their support of this segment of the clothing industry has provided those of us who do ride with a wider choice of materials and styles than we might ever have thought possible.

Many of the clothes I'm wearing in this book come from DeeCee, a division of Washington Manufacturing Company, which doesn't even maintain a catalog because their line is so extensive it would be nearly impossible to illustrate.

Your selection of shirts and jeans will, of course, be in line with your preferred brands, but for general use I doubt you'll find much better than the standard heavyweight jeans and either denim or chambray shirts. These wear well and don't show grime easily, while also being quite comfortable. I prefer the chambray shirts for wear on warmer days, while either chamois cloth flannel or denim shirts are preferable for use in colder weather. For show wear, the variety of body shirts, dress jeans, and so on is extremely varied and often quite gaudy.

As to jeans, I prefer a mildly flared leg over the straight-leg styles, for it provides more freedom around the top of my boot and at the knee. I wear my jeans over my boot tops, so the freedom is needed. Anyone preferring to tuck the jeans in his boots would probably prefer the straight-leg style.

Boots—ah, the romance of the cowboy boot. Again, more people are buying cowboy boots than will ever ride horses, and some of the extremes of style and exotic leathers are, to put it mildly, laughable. Cowboy boots developed over many years, and in some ways are still in a development stage, though now the development tends to be more decorative than useful. I have to agree that today's more rounded toe styles are more comfortable than the old needle toes, but beyond that I can see little real improvement. Peanut brittle or ostrich leathers don't make a useful riding boot, necessarily, but they surely can add to the price of the boot. I guess in some quarters expensive cowboy boots must be a strong status symbol, for there is no other reason on earth for paying upwards of $350 a pair for them with so many good brands available at about one-tenth that price.

I will admit to having one pair of fairly fancy Justin boots that retail for upwards of $100, but the styling is not extreme, except for heel height and leg height, and they are very comfortable during riding, in fact, my most comfortable riding boot, because of the extra features I requested.

The boots have a 14-inch top, in deference to my leg length, and the heel is almost 2½ inches high, with a good undersling. The 14-inch top provides good leg protection, and is still short enough not to cause excessive lower leg heating during warm weather, while the high heel will allow me to ram my feet well into the stirrups should my mount decide to spend a bit of time reaching heights I don't expect. As a not so incidental point, that is just what the high heels on cowboy boots are for, not for anything else. The high arch and the high heel allow you to slam your foot deep into the stirrup without much worry about your foot going on through and making a trap of the stirrup. This is one of the reasons I don't care much for today's trend to low arches and low heels in so-called cowboy boots. Those things are often little better than a pair of shoes when you're on a bouncing horse.

The heel undersling also serves a purpose in that it allows you to slide along the ground a bit should you get a horse that hauls back on its lead rope. The high heel is *not* meant to be planted in the ground in an effort to snub a horse with a lariat, and, should you try to do so, you are almost sure to find yourself getting yanked right out of your tracks, and possibly out of your boots. That underslung heel allows you to skid along, forcing the horse to drag your weight over whatever distance you choose to keep a hold on the rope—not far, I hope.

Steel arch supports and pegged soles make for a high-quality boot, and most today have what is called a Goodyear welt construction that provides good strength and service.

The more or less sharply pointed toe is meant to make it easier to start a foot into the stirrup. Stitching across the instep and up the sides of the boots started out as a means of strengthening the leather in these areas, and now serves double duty as decoration.

In other words, a proper cowboy boot will actually contribute to comfort and safety during a ride, so a careful selection, no matter the price range, is essential. There's certainly a wide enough range to select from.

One other point: I would avoid those boots made with a polyurethane leg. I've had one pair and will never have another. If the plastic starts out not fitting the leg properly, it stays that way, while leather will eventually conform to your leg. Too, the plastic doesn't breathe as leather does, so you will end up with a hotter foot and leg. The savings of six or eight bucks just isn't worth the compromise in quality.

Western clothing items also include hats. Today most Western hats are more decorative than useful, though for someone who spends a lot of time on trails a good hat is a sunshade, a rain deflector, and may serve as a feedbag for your horse, among other things. Unfortunately, the prices of good felt hats continue to rise each year, and I'm not at all convinced that quality standards even reach those of a decade ago when prices were much, much lower. Certainly I've been unable to locate any industry-wide standard, though the use of X as a quality designator is widespread. In essence, a 3X hat is not as good as a 10X, but the 10X from one maker may only equal a 5X from another.

Prices tend to be high, with the 4X hats hitting $50 these days, and the 10X models going for over $100. I have no recommendation to make here because of the diversity of quality and the lack of a real standard. Suffice it to say that spending over $40 or so is probably a waste of money.

Chaps are another item that can prove essential in certain areas. They are also essential for meeting costume requirements in many events. Two styles are generally to be found, with the most popular being the shotgun-style with straight legs. These are usually fringed and can be found in a wide price range (about $55 to $350) depending on how fancy you wish to get. For general brush riding, a plain or mildly fringed pair is best. Batwing chaps conjure up a picture of 1920s Western movies, but are actually more practical for many kinds of really heavy brush riding than are the closer-fitting shotgun chaps.

They are seldom found in show styles, are made of heavier leather, and will outlast most shotgun chaps, while being a bit lower in cost.

Spurs are optional in most shows, but just the same can be found in a variety of styles and types. For practical use, a pair of spurs is a cuing device for your horse, and should have blunted rowels at least an inch in diameter. Show spurs can be had in engraved, silver-filled styles, in brass, blued steel, you name it. Matching bit and spur sets are available, and again the price range is wide, with a practical pair of push-on spurs often found for under $10 and a truly fancy pair of silver filigreed show spurs costing as much as $175, sometimes more.

There is little point in cataloging the various types of Western ties, gloves, and other gear to be found today. While the gloves are essentials to cold-weather riding and some forms of equine groundwork, bolo ties and their counterparts are nothing more than show equipment. Many classes require them, so you'll need to find yourself one if you plan to show in dress classes.

Horse blankets and other items are special needs, and are of concern, generally, only to clipped horses in winter, and to horses that may be ill. Weights vary from light to very heavy, and prices also vary from light to very heavy.

If you feel your horse needs a blanket, most experts seem to prefer the New Zealand style, but in any case make sure the attachments are secure and that the breast and rump straps are strong enough to prevent the horse's pulling the blanket off

Fig. 112. Note the blunted rowels on these spurs.

too easily. Beyond that, select the weight that seems proper for the weather in your region and you should be home free.

TACK CARE

As expensive as it is, good tack remains good for only a short time if it isn't taken care of. Because of the cost, proper care of saddles and bridles is only sensible, especially since the care is not really difficult and consumes relatively small amounts of time.

As you unbox your new saddle and take it out, the smell of leather wafts upwards, but you'll quickly notice several things. The saddle is squeaky and, when hung so the stirrups are in place, the stirrups point in directions that your feet don't.

The second thing a new, or new-to-you, saddle will need is a good oiling with neatsfoot oil or a conditioner such as Lexol. The first thing it needs is to have the stirrup leathers soaked with water.

Yes, soaked with water. The saddle should have all rigging except for the stirrups removed (cinch, rear girth, etc.). Use a bucket of warm water and a sponge to soak the stirrup leathers upwards for a foot to sixteen inches (the stirrups should first be roughly adjusted to your length) depending on how far down they are adjusted. The saddle, during the soaking, must be on a rack, which is fairly easily built if you don't wish to buy one.

Now, take a mop handle or broom handle and turn the stirrups so that they point forward and insert the handle through both stirrups. Once the leather has dried, your stirrups will point in the proper direction; some companies offer metal stirrup hangers made to do this job, but I haven't used them and no one I know has, so I can't comment on whether they're good or bad.

Once the stirrup leathers are dry, the saddle is given a moderate coat of oil or conditioner, in as many places as you can reach. If you use neatsfoot oil, avoid getting any of it on the padded seat. Let the saddle dry again, and then apply a lighter coat. Much of the new saddle squeak will now be gone, and the leather will have a richer tone.

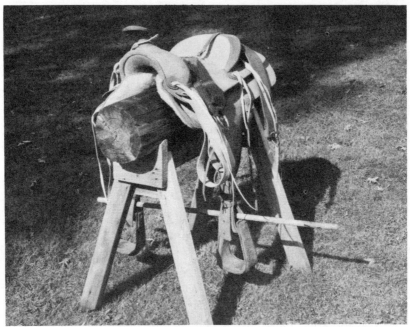

Fig. 113. The stick to turn stirrups can be inserted through the leathers, as shown, or through the stirrups.

Fig. 114. Before oiling your saddle, remove the rigging.

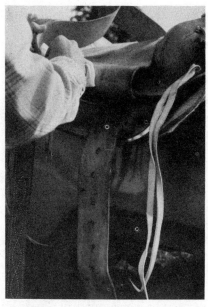

Fig. 115. Make sure all the hard-to-reach places are coated with neatsfoot oil or conditioner.

Most conditioners and neatsfoot oil contain the information that they're not for use on suede and roughout leathers. In fact, what they'll do is tend to mat the fibers down, so the process of smoothing roughout leather is accelerated. Personally, I don't care that much about looks. Since endurance is more important, I go ahead and use oil on my roughout saddle, both sides, and on my roughout boots.

Take care not to get the conditioner or oil on the sheepskin lining of the saddle.

Every so often, any saddle will need a good cleaning and a rigging check to make sure everything is still safe and ready to go. First, remove all rigging and straps, and get out the saddle soap. Use a sponge to work up a good lather with the saddle soap and as little water as will work, and wash off any mud, grit, sweat, and other stains well. If you have a stamped saddle, you'll probably need a soft bristled brush to get down in the swirls and decorative trim. Again, don't get the sheepskin lining of the saddle wet.

Allow the saddle to dry, on its rack and away from any strong source of heat. Then apply a light coat of oil or conditioner to the saddle, working it into the grain side of the leather. After the saddle has dried for something over a half hour, you can go back and wipe off any excess oil.

Rigging is also cleaned at this time, in the same way. Your rigging will probably need more frequent cleaning than will the saddle itself for it is more heavily in contact with your horse, so it picks up more salts from the sweat.

Whether or not you wax the saddle after cleaning is a matter of personal choice, but if you do use a good-quality leather wax or a light coat of saddle soap (no water this time). Both can be buffed out rather well.

Your rigging check actually starts with the saddle itself. Look the horn cap and horn over for wear, checking to see that all stitching is intact. Check the seat for wear of both the seat leather and the stitching, and make a quick check of the cantle. Check all lacing on the saddle and replace any that is badly worn. On the skirts, check the stitching, and then flop the saddle and check the sheepskin lining for wear and any possible tears.

When checking the front rigging, look for frayed stitching or worn cinch strands at any point where they come in contact with the stirrup leathers or fenders. Any broken strands in the cinch should be replaced immediately, as should any broken buckles and other straps. Check the rear rigging for worn stitching, broken buckles, and so on.

If the stirrup coverings are wearing a lot, you can change the near-side and offside stirrups to increase wear, effectively doubling the time you can go without having to either have the stirrups recovered or to buy new ones. Some stirrup styles may be reversed on their regular sides.

Keep special watch on the stirrup leathers for cracks in the leather and excessive wear. This is a safety check, as having a stirrup leather break off doesn't make for skilled riding.

If you store your saddle on a rack that supports at least the upper parts of the skirts, it will last a great deal longer.

Bridle care is similar to saddle care, but needs to be done at least as frequently as the rigging is done, for the bridle leather is constantly in contact with the horse, and thus is easily damaged by sweat.

Fig. 116. Is it any wonder I like Lexol? Jim's old show saddle was needed for photos, but he hadn't even had time to look at it in a couple of years. Mildew (see the stirrup on the right) was exceptionally heavy, but a single wipe on and wipe off of Lexol gave the results seen on the left.

Rein care depends on the type of reins you use. Mine are simply washed in Woolite when dirty. Leather reins need oil or conditioner to stay in good shape.

A too-often overlooked part of tack care is the cleaning of the bit. Wash the bit in a dishwashing detergent, rinse it well, and then dry it. Your horse doesn't care for a dirty, slobber-caked bit in its mouth any more than you would.

Chaps need cleaning and conditioning depending on use, too. Generally, a good leather brush will get the suede styles reasonably clean, so that then all you need do is apply a conditioner to the flesh side of the leather (in this case, I would use a conditioner such as Lexol rather than neatsfoot oil for a very simple reason: it smells better).

Boots. Care of boots is important, and I always start a new pair with a good dose of Lexol, followed by, for smooth leather, a good waxing. The Lexol treatment is repeated as often as needed, though the shine may be neglected if I'm too busy to waste time. Lexol is preferred for boot treatment over neatsfoot oil because the leather will still take a coat of polish and reward your buffing efforts with a shine. Boots probably wear out faster from the effects of acids in urine and manure than from actual working or riding. Keeping them clean helps, and keeping a good bit of conditioner on the boots means you can turn a hose on them and brush vigorously without having to worry a great deal about the effect the water will have on the leather.

7. FEEDING YOUR HORSE

The subject of equine nutrition is a complex one in some respects, and the availability of feeds of different types varies somewhat from area to area (not as much as formerly, for such things as brewer's mash are becoming available, in bagged form, in regions far from any brewery). Still, some forms of pasture won't grow well in certain areas, while certain types of hays are more easily found in some parts of the country.

The real complexity comes more with the needs of the individual horse, though, for a horse is superlatively sensitive to amounts and types of feed, to the point where a large variety of equine problems can be almost eliminated by proper feeding.

Proper feeding starts with a consideration of the digestive system of the horse. For its size, the horse has a small stomach, and a single stomach, which means that it can't fill one stomach and bring the food back for later enjoyment as can a ruminant such as a deer or cow. It also means that the stomach won't hold enough to keep the hunger pangs down for very long, so that continual feeding is the horse's nature. With its grazing habits in a natural state, this works well, for the foods are not concentrates. But much of what today's horse gets for feed is concentrated, in the forms of grains such as oats or corn, and even in pelletized hays and other nutrients.

Because overeating can cause many problems, today's horse must be fed specific amounts and must be kept from getting more than those amounts when food concentrates are used. Thus the recommendation for totally secure grain storage (legume hays such as alfalfa should also be stored securely, as they are natural forms of concentrated nutrients). A horse's grazing habits will lead it to continue feeding even when nutritional needs are met, for it has no way of identifying the actual nutrient content of feeds.

When you buy your horse, the previous owner should be able to supply you with a base point for feeding. A look at the horse can quickly tell you if this base point is a good one: a healthy, well-fed horse will have a glossy coat, be well muscled and alert, but will not be fat (assuming some conditioning or enough exercise). If the base point supplied doesn't seem to be doing well for your horse, then you'll need to work from a standard. For light horse breeds, a standard is a horse of about 1,000 pounds, standing from 14-2 to 15-2, though the variations on this are wide and frequent. Working feed amounts for the 1,000-pound horse is fairly easy. Taking the weight of your own horse and developing your feed standards in relation to its weight in comparison to the standard is also fairly easy. If your horse weighs about 1,100 pounds, simply add 10 percent to the amounts of nutrients supplied. If your horse is smaller, say 750 pounds, substract about 25 percent.

Too, the intensity of work is a factor to be considered. Just as with people, the horse that gets a lot of exercise needs more food than does the stable-bound steed that works only a few minutes a day. Placing a stable-bound horse on the same diet as a working horse will assure you of a fat and not very healthy animal. You are doing your horses no favor by letting them eat too much, just as humans do themselves no favor by eating too much.

Parasites of the internal variety can also be a factor in nutrition. If your horse is full of worms, you're going to be putting as much money into feeding the worms as you are into feeding the horse, and you'll still have a poorly fed and lethargic animal.

Because internal parasites are always present in horses, a major portion of the chapter on horse diseases and first aid will cover parasitology. A proper and constant worming program is essential to the continuing health of every horse. And, while good wormers aren't cheap, the savings in feed not wasted, plus the probable savings in vet bills, will more than pay the cost of the program.

Nutrition, naturally, starts with nutrients, and these are probably best started with proteins. Crude protein is the total amount of protein in the feed, while digestible protein is the amount of that crude protein your horse can actually utilize. So that means your horse will get, for example, 17.3 percent crude protein in alfalfa (assuming it is of good quality and cut at the pre- or early bloom stage), and can utilize 10 percent of the total weight of the alfalfa fed as protein. Of course, protein is far from the whole nutrient story, as calcium, phosphorus, carotene, and other substances are necessary, and sometimes, though not always, present. Alfalfa is a simple example of a full nutrient because it provides 50 percent of its weight as total digestible nutrients and includes all the nutrients mentioned above. Good-quality alfalfa may reach up to, or even a bit over, 20 percent protein, while hays such as timothy and orchard grass seldom reach above 7 percent. Basically, this means that while alfalfa may seem a more expensive hay to feed, it can work out to a bit less (at this moment, orchard grass hay around here is going for about $1.50 a bale, while alfalfa sells for about $2.25 to $2.50, not even double the price for nearly three times the nutritional value).

No matter the kind of hay you buy, you must keep a careful check on hay quality. The earlier a hay is cut, the better its quality will normally be. Late-cut hay will have a lot of stems and fewer leaves. Stems provide very little value in the form of nutrition, so check the hay carefully. Also check the hay for excessive dust—some horses are allergic to dusty feeds—and mold. Moldy hay of any kind cannot be fed to horses for it causes nervous-system damage and can very easily either kill the horse outright or force you to have it put down.

In general, your horse will require a diet of 12 to 13 percent protein (nursing mares need a diet with about 21 percent), at least two ounces of salt, 70 grams of calcium, 60 grams of phosphorus, 68 grams of potassium, 6.4 grams of magnesium, 640 milligrams of iron, 400 mg. of zinc, 340 mg. of manganese, 90 mg. of copper, 2.6 mg. of iodine, and 1.5 mg. of cobalt. From there, we move to general vitamin requirements: vitamin A needs are about 50,000 international units; vitamin D, about 7,000 IU; vitamin E, 200 IU; choline, 400 mg.; pantothentic acid, 60 mg.; niacin, 50 mg.; riboflavin, 40 mg.; thiamin, 25 mg.; vitamin K, 8 mg.; folic acid, 2.5 mg.; and vitamin B12, 125 micrograms.

You need to allow about 2½ pounds of feed per day per hundred pounds of bodyweight for your horse: the figures are designed to be a base for a 1,000-pound animal, as we said.

Lack of calcium or phosphorus, or both, is sometimes a problem with horses, so that knowledge of the basic content in various feeds can be a help. Cereal grains are low in calcium, while protein supplements of animal origin are high. Cereal grains are rich in phosphorus, but a large percentage of the mineral is not readily available as a nutrient. Most protein-rich feed supplements are high in phosphorus, but, as with cereal grains, it is often not available as a nutrient since it is in what is known as bound form. Plant calcium and phosphorus levels can be upgraded by using the proper fertilizers.

I see little point in going into just why each of the nutrients is essential to the health of your horse. That information is readily available in many places, and doesn't change the facts that your horse does need the nutrients, in balanced amounts, and that the nutrients are available in various forms.

HAYS

Most likely you'll end up feeding hay grown nearby, as that is usually cheapest and most easily obtained. Whenever possible, you will be wise to select a couple of different types of hays so you can give your horse a taste break sometime during the course of hay feeding.

Alfalfa is a legume hay, as are clovers and lespedeza. These are tops in protein content and high in calcium, but deficient in phosphorus, which means that you'll almost always need to feed a phosphorus supplement to balance the nutrient ratios. The legume hays are usually fed in combination with a grass hay so that a medium level of protein is attained. It is becoming a normal thing for horsemen to feed legume hays alone, assuming the horse's kidneys are in normal shape (an excess of protein over the body's needs increases the work the kidneys have to do). Too, if the horse has been on a grass hay diet, or pastured, the change to legume hays must be made gradually. Actually, this last applies to all changes in any horse's diet; they must be made gradually to prevent the sort of systemic shock that brings on laminitis.

Grass hays include brome, timothy, bermuda, orchard grass, and others. Generally, the protein content is much lower than for legume hays, as are the calcium and phosphorus contents.

PASTURES

Pasturing a horse allows it, at least in part, to eat in a more natural manner and can serve to reduce feed costs where it is available. The grasses used for pasture will vary with region, soil types, and so on. Cool season permanent pastures in my area often combine several grasses, seeded at different rates per acre. A favorite is Kentucky bluegrass, which grows to about seven inches and, because of its root system type, is good at healing over torn-up spots. Fescue is also frequently used, but is not as highly favored by horses, as it seems to be lacking in taste qualities. Still, the use is extensive, at least in part because it grows easily in many soil conditions.

Orchard grass makes pasture as well as hay fields and provides good feed value and high yields; it is usually combined with bluegrass and one of the clovers. White clover is a legume and holds up well under heavy grazing. Ladino clover is a larger variety of white clover and works in well with the taller grasses (fescue, orchard grass). Bermuda grass is a good pasture grass for hot, dry times of the year, while small grains often make good winter pastures (rye, barley).

Care must be used when turning horses out during the first months of spring pasture growth, when the growing plants are lush and heavy with water. The over-rich grass allowed to be eaten after a winter on dry feed will almost certainly tempt your horse to overeat and can easily led to laminitis. Any horse turned out on fresh, spring pasture should be limited to no more than about fifteen minutes of feeding per day for a couple of weeks.

As I have already mentioned, checking hay before buying it is essential. Poor-quality hay makes poor feed, and some forms of hay are actually dangerous to horses, so over-emphasis is just about impossible on this point. There are about six points to watch for when buying hay.

1. Check to make sure the hay is leafy, as most of the nutrients are in the leaf.

2. Look for weeds and trash plants of other kinds in the hay and reject it if there is very much.

3. Look for a bright green color. The green shows the hay was cured properly and also indicates, if it is fresh cut, that vitamin A content will be high.

4. Make sure there are not a lot of woody, thick stems.

5. Be absolutely sure any hay used is free of mold and excessive dust. Musty, moldy hay should be destroyed or used for compost in an area where your horse cannot possibly get to it.

6. Each type of hay will have a slightly different odor, but it will smell clean and fresh if it is clean and fresh.

Hay cut in the early stages of maturity is best, and this is usually shown by the leafiness; as hay matures, the stems get longer and thicker and the leaves drop off more easily.

CONCENTRATES

Before feeding concentrates, you'll want to check local feed prices. It's sometimes possible to supplement hays with concentrates without adding a great deal to the overall cost of feeding, which will definitely have an effect on the kind of concentrate you decide to use.

Oats can generally be classed as the preferred horse feed in this country, for the price is usually reasonable, and the nutritional values suit horses very well. Hulled oats are heavier per bushel and may be listed as rolled or crimped. Crude protein content is about 13 percent, with crude fiber making up another 12 percent, calcium 11 percent, and phosphorus 39 percent. Look for the heaviest oats possible (over thirty-two pounds per bushel is best) for these have the least amount of hull, and are most easily digested.

Out West a lot of people prefer barley to oats, and it is another grain with about 13 percent crude protein and the same amount of crude fiber. Barley fed to horses must be ground, or steamrolled, and it is usually fed in combination with oats or another, more bulky feed, with barley making up about 75 percent of the total when used with oats.

Corn is a fine horse feed, with just under 10½ percent crude protein, but it is a bit low on crude fiber (about 2½ percent). Corn is also deficient in some minerals, particularly calcium. I've seen corn fed in so many different ways it kind of makes me wonder whether there'll ever be a standard. One farmer simply feeds it on the cob, while another uses cracked corn, and some feed it whole. Of course, corn on the cob is cheapest, while each operation increases the expense of the feed.

Wheat bran provides a slight laxative effect and is quite high in crude protein (somewhere around 16 percent). It is a bulky feed since it is made up of the outer covering of the wheat kernel, and that bulk, along with its laxative property, is of value in feeding horses.

Generally, you can figure the total digestive nutrient value of most grain concentrates at about 75 percent of the total, but the figure can drop way off if a lot of hull is in the grain.

Milo is a grain similar to corn in overall nutritional value, though the crude protein is higher at about 12½ percent. It should never be fed whole as the kernel is extremely hard and nearly indigestible in the equine stomach.

Because of the variation in the weight of a bushel, it is best that you feed all grains by weight. The weight of a bushel of oats may vary from twenty-three to about thirty-five or even thirty-six pounds, and simply scooping out a couple of quarts is not a good idea.

Supplements to add overall protein or improve protein quality are needed for most horses at least part of the time. Soybean meal offers 44 percent crude protein and 32 percent calcium with 67 percent phosphorus, while linseed meal has 38 percent protein. Cottonseed meal has 41 percent crude protein, while dried skim milk has 35 percent.

As you can easily see, these supplements are a lot higher in protein content than grains or hays, no matter their type. The supplements are more expensive than either grains or hays because of the higher protein content, and you may be somewhat tempted to cut back because of the price. While overnutrition is as bad as undernutrition, cutting back too far on protein is going to result in a poorly conditioned horse and, most likely, one subject to all kinds of ills.

In addition to grains and natural supplements, many companies are now making complete feeds available in bagged form. Each of these feeds is different, so you need to check the label to determine the varying protein, calcium, phosphorus, and other nutrient percentages.

TREATING THE HORSE

At one time or another most of us treat our horses. The point is that the treat should be one with nutrient value and not just a couple of sugar cubes fed only for the animal's pleasure. A small apple or two, some carrots, even a potato provide good total digestive nutrients. They can be used as rewards for some success in training—anything that keeps the horse working willingly is a good idea, but take care when feeding treats as a reward, for the horse may decide to work only if rewarded in such a way.

When carrots are fed, slice them from end to end instead of in chunks so the horse won't choke on them, and, if used as a supplement, mix them in with the feed. If you feed apples as a treat, hold to one or two a day, as apples in excess can too easily cause colic.

Sometimes even a handful of fresh grass from outside a pasture will provide a treat for your horse. Like almost every other animal, what's on the other side of the fence always looks better than what's inside the fence—you'll note that pastured horses will, whenever possible, manage to get their heads down and clear a strip along the outside of any fence (I've seen horses delicately arch their necks over an electric fence to work on a strip, and others slip their heads through the rails of post and rail fences; a few in barbed wire—not recommended at all for horse fencing—will even push down the top strand to get at grass outside the fence).

Generally, feeding by hand is not considered a good practice, but, to be honest, I think most people do so at least once in a while. Not making a habit of the hand feeding is the most sensible thing, as well as using the correct technique in holding the food (arch your hand so the treat stands up where the horse doesn't have to nibble at your fingers for it).

Hand feeding is said to turn horses into nibblers, but I haven't seen it happen when the practice is not overdone. I think it's more likely the horse becomes a nibbler because it is bored, either with its life or its feed or both, and thus paying attention causes it to use its mouth to demand more attention. If you feed your horse properly and give it some affection and attention, as well as normal care on a regular basis, it should not turn into a nibbler or biter.

To ease up on the chore of programming nutrition for your horse, I've included several tables that give the nutrient requirements for horses ranging in weight from 440 to 1,320 pounds. Also, the tables include average feed compositions, but you must remember that these are averages. According to the people who supplied the table, the best method of determining feed composition is to have it analyzed. Your local extension agent can either provide or direct you to this service at a moderate cost.

The tables used are from a presentation given by Dr. J. P. Fontenot of Virginia Polytechnic Institute and State University, Blacksburg, Virginia, and were supplied by Dr. Arden Huff of the same state university.

Feeding sequence is of as great importance as are feed amounts. As a minimum, your horse should be fed at least twice a day, preferably three times daily, when stabled. Grain is normally fed first, with the hay following, and there should be a breakdown that sees your horse getting more of the roughage (hay) at night than in the morning and noon feedings. Because horses learn to wait for mealtimes, it is best to maintain as

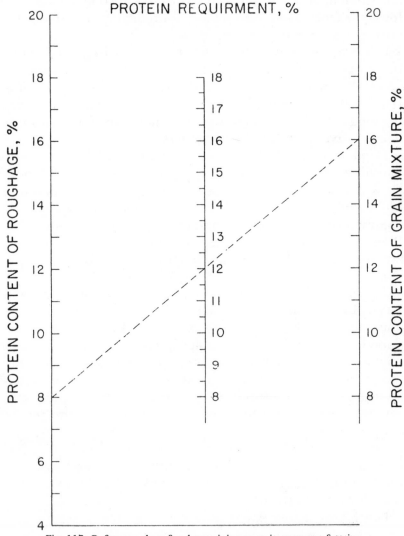

Fig. 117. Reference chart for determining protein content of grains.

Fig. 118. NUTRIENT REQUIREMENTS OF MATURE HORSES, PREGNANT MARES, AND LACTATING MARES[a] (DAILY NUTRIENTS PER ANIMAL)

Body Weight lb.	Daily feed[c] lb.	Digestible energy Mcal	TDN lb.	Protein lb.	Digestible protein lb.	Vitamin A[b] 1000 I.U.	Calcium lb.	Phosphorus lb.
Mature Horses at Rest (Maintenance)								
440	7.3	8.2	4.1	0.66	0.35	5.0	0.018	0.013
880	12.3	13.9	6.9	1.11	0.59	10.0	0.035	0.026
1100	14.6	16.4	8.2	1.31	0.70	12.5	0.044	0.033
1320	16.7	18.8	9.4	1.50	0.80	15.0	0.053	0.040
Mature Horses at Light Work (2 hr./day)								
440	9.3	10.4	5.2	0.84	0.44	5.0	0.018	0.013
880	16.3	18.4	9.2	1.48	0.78	10.0	0.035	0.026
1100	19.5	21.9	10.9	1.77	0.93	12.5	0.044	0.033
1320	22.6	25.4	12.7	2.05	1.08	15.0	0.053	0.040
Mature Horses at Medium Work (2 hr./day)								
440	11.7	13.2	6.6	1.06	0.56	5.0	0.020	0.015
880	21.1	23.8	11.9	1.92	1.01	10.0	0.038	0.029
1100	25.5	28.7	14.3	2.30	1.22	12.5	0.047	0.035
1320	29.9	33.6	16.8	2.70	1.43	15.0	0.055	0.042
Mares, Last 90 Days of Pregnancy								
440	7.7	8.7	4.4	0.80	0.48	10.0	0.023	0.018
880	13.2	14.9	7.4	1.35	0.82	20.0	0.043	0.033
1100	15.4	17.4	8.7	1.60	0.95	25.0	0.053	0.040
1320	17.7	20.0	10.0	1.84	1.10	30.0	0.062	0.046
Mares, Peak of Lactation								
440	13.5	15.2	7.6	1.65	1.06	10.0	0.075	0.051
880	21.8	24.4	12.2	2.60	1.65	20.0	0.092	0.078
1100	24.6	27.6	13.8	2.90	1.82	25.0	0.103	0.085
1320	26.7	30.0	15.0	3.09	1.93	30.0	0.141	0.095

[a]Adapted from N.R.C. 1973. Nutrient Requirements of Domestic Animals, No. 6. Nutrient Requirements of Horses, National Research Council, Washington, D.C.

[b]One mg. beta carotene equals 400 I.U. vitamin A.

[c]Air dry feed.

Fig. 119. COMPOSITION OF FEEDS FOR HORSES[a]

Kind of feed	Dry matter %	Digestible energy Mcal./lb.	TDN %	Protein %	Digestible protein %	Calcium %	Phosphorus %	Carotene mg./lb.
Roughages								
Alfalfa hay	89.2	0.91	51	15.3	9.8	1.20	0.20	13.5
Red clover hay	90.1	0.89	50	12.8	7.5	1.31	0.21	14.3
Orchardgrass hay	88.3	0.75	41	8.1	3.8	0.40	0.20	6.8
Timothy hay	88.4	0.78	43	7.3	3.2	0.36	0.17	4.3
Oat hay	88.2	0.79	43	8.1	4.0	0.23	0.21	40.5
Crimson clover hay	87.4	0.87	48	14.8	9.5	1.24	0.16	13.9
Fescue hay	88.5	0.79	43	9.3	4.7	0.44	0.32	8.4
Lespedeza hay	93.2	0.88	48	12.5	7.0	0.97	0.21	—
Corn cobs	90.4	0.50	26	2.5	.0	0.11	0.04	—
Grains and other high energy feeds								
Barley grain	89.0	1.48	74	11.6	7.3	0.08	0.42	0.
Corn grain	89.0	1.62	81	8.9	4.7	0.02	0.27	—
Oats grain	89.0	1.25	62	11.7	7.4	0.06	0.29	—
Sugarcane molasses	75.0	1.09	54	3.2	.0	0.89	0.08	—
Wheat grain	89.0	1.57	78	12.7	8.4	0.12	0.30	0.6
Corn and cob meal	87.0	1.39	68	8.1	4.0	0.04	0.27	—
Wheat middlings	89.0	1.52	76	18.0	13.4	0.08	0.52	—
Wheat bran	89.0	1.04	58	16.0	11.5	0.14	1.17	
Protein supplements								
Soybean meal	89.0	1.43	71	45.8	39.8	0.32	0.67	—
Dried skim milk	94.0	1.54	77	32.0	—	1.21	0.99	—
Linseed meal	91.0	1.38	69	35.1	29.6	0.40	0.83	—
Mineral supplements								
Dicalcium phosphate	96.0	—	—	—	—	22.20	17.90	—
Limestone	100.0	—	—	—	—	35.84	—	—

[a]As fed basis.

Fig. 120. PROTEIN REQUIREMENTS OF GROWING HORSES[a]

Age	Body wt.	Percentage of mature weight	Daily feed per animal[b]	Requirement	
				Total protein	Digestible protein
mo.	lb.		lb.	%	%
440 lb. Mature Wt.					
3	132	25.0	7.2	16.1	11.7
6	198	45.0	7.6	13.4	9.2
12	297	67.5	7.1	10.5	6.4
18	363	82.5	7.2	9.6	5.6
42	440	100.0	7.3	9.0	4.8
880 lb. Mature Wt.					
3	187	21.3	9.3	17.6	13.1
6	374	42.5	11.0	12.8	8.6
12	572	65.0	12.1	10.9	6.8
18	726	82.5	12.5	10.1	5.9
42	880	100.0	12.3	9.0	4.8
1100 lb. Mature Wt.					
3	242	22.0	10.7	17.1	12.7
6	495	45.0	13.7	12.1	8.6
12	713	65.0	14.9	11.1	6.9
18	880	80.0	15.3	10.2	6.0
42	1100	100.0	14.6	9.0	4.8
1320 lb. Mature Wt.					
3	308	23.3	12.6	16.7	12.3
6	583	44.2	15.3	12.5	8.3
12	847	64.1	16.8	11.0	6.8
18	1056	80.0	17.1	10.0	5.9
42	1320	100.0	16.7	9.0	4.8

[a]Adapted from N.R.C. 1973. Nutrient Requirements of Domestic Animals, No. 6. Nutrient Requirements of Horses, National Research Council, Washington, D.C.
[b]Air dry feed.

regular a schedule for each feeding as is possible. Don't feed at 5 A.M. one morning and at 8 A.M. the next, if it's avoidable.

Make no sudden changes in diet. That's not to say you shouldn't make dietary changes if your horse isn't doing as well as you wish on the feed program in use, but make any changes gradually, taking, for instance, a week to increase the oat ration from ten pounds to sixteen pounds as you increase the work your horse is doing.

Don't feed anything other than roughage to a hot horse, and then only a small amount. Actually, it's best to cool a horse down before feeding him anything.

Fig. 121. PROTEIN REQUIREMENTS OF MATURE HORSES, PREGNANT MARES, AND LACTATING MARES[a]

Body wt.	Daily feed per animal[b]	Requirement	
		Total protein	Digestible protein
lb.	lb.	%	%
Mature Horses at Rest (Maintenance)			
440	7.3	9.0	4.8
880	12.3	9.0	4.8
1100	14.6	9.0	4.8
1320	16.7	9.0	4.8
Mature Horses at Light Work (2 hr./day)			
440	9.3	9.0	4.8
880	16.3	9.0	4.8
1100	19.5	9.0	4.8
1320	22.6	9.0	4.8
Mature Horses at Medium Work (2 hr./day)			
440	11.7	9.0	4.8
880	21.1	9.0	4.8
1100	25.5	9.0	4.8
1320	29.9	9.0	4.8
Mares, Last 90 Days of Pregnancy			
440	7.7	10.4	6.2
880	13.2	10.4	6.2
1100	15.4	10.4	6.2
1320	17.7	10.4	6.2
Mares, Peak of Lactation			
440	13.5	12.2	7.8
880	21.8	12.0	7.6
1100	24.6	11.8	7.5
1320	26.7	11.6	7.2

[a]Adapted from N.R.C. 1973. Nutrient Requirements of Domestic Animals, No. 6. Nutrient Requirements of Horses, National Research Council, Washington, D.C.
[b]Air dry feed.

Keep a check on the feedbox and the floor around and under it. Watch your horse eat a few times; if he is a feed bolter, you may wish to get some baseball-sized rocks and place them in the manger. Using clean rocks in this way makes the horse feel around for the feed and keeps down any chance of his bolting it. If you keep a watch on the feedbox, you'll notice when your horse goes off his feed and can start looking for reasons.

Keep the manger and water bucket, or waterer, clean.

Don't water a hot horse, but make sure your horse has water available at all other times. The average horse will need about a dozen gallons of water a day and is best served if the water is more or less constantly available.

During cold weather, your horse will probably drink a bit less water (and more during very hot weather), but it will still need large amounts. Waterers should be maintained at a temperature of about 45° F. so that ice doesn't form.

In most cases, salt can be fed free choice. Very few horses overdo on salt, but a great many don't get enough. Salt can be fed in block form or loose and can be bought plain or with a variety of minerals added. If your roughage shows up low in minerals, select a salt block, or loose salt, that contains those minerals lacking in other feeds.

Switch off feeds occasionally, going from, for example, straight timothy or orchard-grass hay to a mixture of alfalfa and the other hay (make the change gradually, of course), so that your horse won't get tired of the same old taste and go off its feed.

Nutritionally related diseases and problems are many, with some of them being extremely serious, so proper feeding is essential. Your horse will be better off if you work with feeds that have been analyzed for content or have their contents listed on the label. Even then, keeping an eye on your horse is always a good idea, so that you detect nutritional problems when they begin.

NUTRITIONAL PROBLEMS

Nutritional anemia is primarily a lack of iron and shows up as the horse loses appetite and becomes thinner and thinner. Advanced cases may result in death. Feeds should be analyzed with an eye to iron, copper, cobalt, and vitamin content. Anemia also may stunt growth in young horses.

Monday-morning disease is less common than it once was, but it still occurs. The primary cause is thought to be maintaining a heavy feed schedule, after taking an idle horse, working it hard, and then allowing it to return to idleness. The signs of Monday-morning disease are a stiff gait, a lot of sweating, lameness, some abdominal pain. The horse may take a sitting position, and finally, simply lie down. You'll seldom if ever find the disease in pastured horses and in horses that are worked consistently.

Colic can be brought on by improper feeding, improper watering, or working the horse too soon after watering or feeding. The horse will, in milder cases, appear to nibble at its sides and abdomen in an effort to still the pain; worse cases will find the horse in such pain that it gets down and rolls, kicking strongly, and this is dangerous. A colic-stricken horse should be kept up and walking, if at all possible, and you should call your vet immediately. The colicky horse will also refuse food and water.

Founder is probably the most easily prevented disease of horses. Most forms, all with the same results, are related to nutrition, while one is related to overwork on hard surfaces. Grass founder is caused by letting a horse out for too long on spring pasture after a winter of dry feed, while overeating and overdrinking can cause other forms. The horse will have extreme pain, usually worse in the front hooves, and will either walk on its heels or refuse to move. Its temperature will rise, possibly as high as 106° F. The condition is brought on by, primarily, improper treatment by the horse's owner, and chronic lameness will result if the condition is continued and will also probably result if the horse is not treated by a vet as soon as possible. If the first case of laminitis is severe, the horse may have to be put down, and, in any case, a horse once foundered is more subject to its happening again.

Heaves are associated with feeding dusty hay. You'll see the flanks jerking and the horse will cough as it appears to have problems in getting air out of its lungs. Treatment simply requires turning the horse out to pasture if possible, or cutting down on dust in the feed (if all hay seems to cause this, you should consider using a pelleted feed for even the roughage portion of your horse's diet).

Goiter is an iodine deficiency and was once a large problem, for animals and humans, around the world. Essentially, the thyroid gland enlarges in an attempt to make sufficient thyroxine (a compound for the formation of which iodine is essential) for the body. Feeding iodized salt prevents the condition.

Rickets is a nutritional disease caused by a lack of vitamin D, calcium, or phosphorus or an improper ratio between the minerals. Rickets is found in young animals and shows up as joint enlargement, with pain, and as irregular beads on the ribs. The disease is treated by making sure the calcium and phosphorus ratio is correct and that the amounts are proper, while supplementing vitamin D, either by turning the animal out in direct sunlight or using vitamin supplements.

Salt deficiency brings on a loss of appetite, will retard growth or cause a loss of weight, and produces a strong appetite for salt. For horses that have been salt starved, you cannot feed salt free choice as they'll eat enough to poison themselves, so hand feeding is recommended until the animal is ready for free access to salt.

Night blindness is brought on by a lack of vitamin A. Continued deficiency of this vitamin may eventually lead to permanent blindness. Easily prevented, night blindness is treated by feeding vitamin A, and keeping the carotene (vitamin A precursor) sources high.

Cribbing, or wood chewing or stump sucking, may or may not be a totally nutritional problem. It may start with a lack of vitamin D or calcium or phosphorus in the diet and then, after the diet is corrected, continue as a vice. Cribbing is also considered to be brought on by a stabled horse's boredom. It is also sometimes called pica. First, treat whatever has caused the symptoms. Check, or have your vet check, for vitamin or mineral deficiencies. Get the horse out of the stable more, pasturing it if possible. Minimize any stress. Feed smaller amounts at more frequent intervals. Feed several extra pounds per day of hay low in nutritional value to keep the horse occupied.

Some other suggestions for relieving your horse's boredom include tying several plastic milk containers where the horse can use its head to move them, as a kind of toy, and providing a goat or other small animal as a companion to the stabled horse.

Generally, most horsemen agree that severe cribbing becomes a nearly impossible-to-break habit, and a cribbing strap may well be needed. Cribbing can cause all kinds of other problems, from colic brought on by air sucked into the stomach, to tooth and other mouth problems.

Sometimes, the selection of barn designs and pastures will help prevent cribbing, and a lot of other problems.

8. STABLES AND PASTURES

As noted in the chapter on nutrition, the type of pasture will vary around the country, as some grasses grow just fine where others won't grow at all and vice versa. Too, the area of pasture needed, if that's to be your horse's main ration, will vary. In a few areas, little more than a couple of acres will be needed, while in others there may not be enough feed for a single horse on six dozen acres. That is a decision to be formed by you on the advice of your extension agent and is also directly related to just how much land you can afford to buy or rent.

If the pasture is large enough, divide it into several fields so that one can recover while another is being used. This also makes it easier to get in a pasture and spread any droppings, which helps fertilize a larger area, keeps the horses from eating certain clumps while leaving others, and helps to cut down on parasite infestations.

Pasture care includes such things as hazard removal. All cans, bottles, and other trash must be removed, as must all boards, and a check should be made for nails and other small metal debris that could be lying about. Check along tree lines for trees with low crotches and remove, at the trunk, one limb of such crotches. More than one good horse has been lost by getting hung up in a forked tree.

Check pasture fencing. Certain types of fence are preferable for horses, and some types are no good at all. Among the latter types is barbed wire, probably the most common type of animal fencing in the country. Certain types of horses seem to never get hurt on barbed wire, but the more hot-blooded breeds, and most foals, should never be enclosed in barbed wire. Sooner or later, they'll be badly cut if they are. Range-wise horses appear to have fewer problems when confronted with barbed wire than do most others, but still it's best to not use the stuff at all.

Metal mesh fencing is expensive, but for paddock use where lengths aren't as long, heavy metal mesh with openings too small to catch a hoof are fine, sturdy, and long lasting.

Wood fencing of many designs is available and is often preferred, for a good wood fence will last thirty years or more, and can be erected by almost anyone at a reasonable cost. Generally the least expensive wood fencing is the type made of pressure-treated lumber, usually pine. Post and rail designs are still extremely popular, but the best for horses is likely to be a board-style fence. Foals can often escape from post and rail fencing, though geldings and mares, unless in heat, will seldom even try unless a rail is down or their care isn't good. Cedar and redwood fencing are also good, but they tend to cost more than twice as much as does pressure-treated wood.

Local varieties of wood can also affect costs. In my area, locust abounds, and it is, overall, about number three on the fence-wood list for durability, untreated, in contact with the ground. In other areas, you may not find any. In a few areas, cedar is readily available at low cost, or, sometimes, for the cutting.

Fencing for horses goes on to the electric fence. Again, this is not preferred over wood, but is often used today. Any electric fence used for horses should be of the mild type, not a "weed-burner" style. The weed burners are fine for thicker-skinned animals, but can severely damage a horse with their higher shock values.

Electric fencing is probably the cheapest way to keep a horse in, but is actually best used to supplement other fencing (as, for example, when you have a stallion penned along a road, inside a wood fence, an electric fence used possibly three or four feet inside the wood fence will keep the stallion away from the wood fence and any questing young hands). Still, for cold-blooded stock horse breeds, a good electric fence, set to just a bit above breast height, will hold most mature horses. It is what I will be fencing with as soon as I finish this book, to hold an older gelding and possibly one younger one.

The shocks are so brief, however, that a skittish horse that has been badly frightened will often zip right on through the fence and not even feel the shock. This can be partially prevented by tying pieces of old sheet every three feet or so along the fence, so the horse can easily see it is there. Usually, the horse will get curious and manage to get shocked within a day or two of being fenced with electric wire. Once that happens, barring accidents, the horse will avoid touching the fence ever again, or at least for a long period of time.

In fact, there are people in my area with horses inside electric fences who turn the fences on only about one week out of six— and never have a horse get loose.

One further comment on electric fences: never use those small fiberglass or metal rods driven in the ground to support the fence. A horse may too easily impale itself on one of those. That actually holds true for any form of horse fencing: posts should never have sharp ends.

STABLES

Any stable that is needed is going to depend on what your land is like, how much severe weather you can expect, and, for size, on the number of horses you have. Basically, though, stabling needs are quite similar for all horses, except for foaling mares (they need twice as much room).

Generally you will need an adequate structure, though it doesn't have to be fancy nor have a lot of unnecessary appointments. In my area, horsemen of many types use many types of barns, but the favorite seems to be pole construction with board and batten siding of oak or pine. (Oak and pine are comparable in price at local lumberyards or sawmills, and oak gives a bit better service if not in contact with the ground.)

Space allowances for stalls start at a minimum of ten feet by twelve feet, though a twelve-foot square is even better. If you

Plan D-6118 is a two-stall pole barn horse stable with a combination tack and feed room. The basic purpose of this plan is to provide the one- or two-horse owner with a stable that has the maximum amount of functional features at low cost. The plan was developed by the American Plywood Association and features the use of plywood throughout.

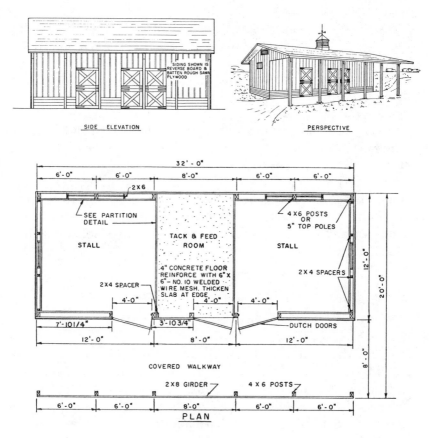

Fig. 122. For most horsemen, a two-stall barn will be more than sufficient, and this, Plan D-6118, is excellent and attractive. Pole construction, along with the use of plywood for siding and stalls, provides for quick and easy erection.

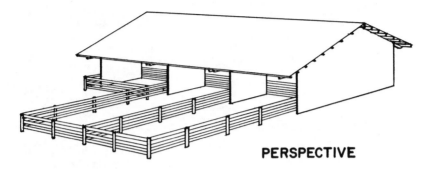

PERSPECTIVE

*Plan D-6107 developed by the Cooperative Plan Exchange, Beltsville, Maryland.

Plan D-6010* is a larger plan designed for eight or more horses. The stalls are placed back-to-back and open to the outside. A 4' roof overhang is provided for protection from the weather. This barn is of pole construction with trussed rafters and a metal roof.

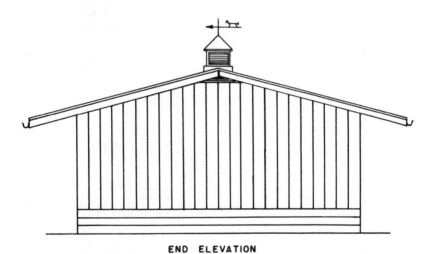

END ELEVATION

Fig. 123. For the person who needs more horses, plan D-6010, developed by the Cooperative Plan Exchange in Beltsville, MD, is easily erected and provides good shelter, while three horses will do extremely well in the barn shown as plan D-6107.

Plan D-6107* is a three-stall pole barn horse stable with the unique feature of outside paddocks for all three stalls. This plan is particularly suited to pleasure horses that are not in training. The outside runs will help the horse get exercise and should contribute to the well-being of the horse. The plan can also be modified to provide conventional box stalls.

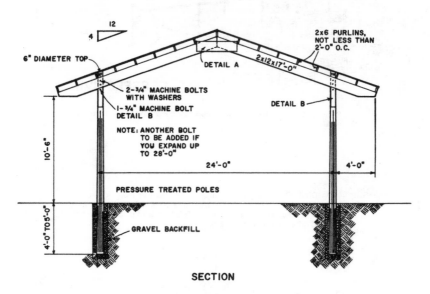

SECTION

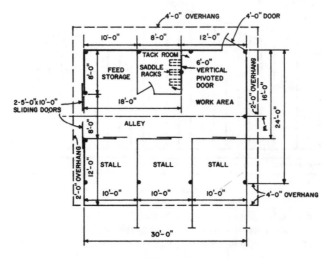

PLAN

Fig. 124. Details and floor plan for D-6107.

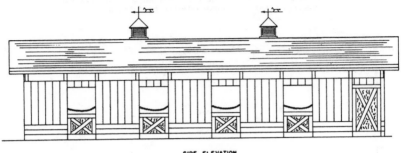

SIDE ELEVATION

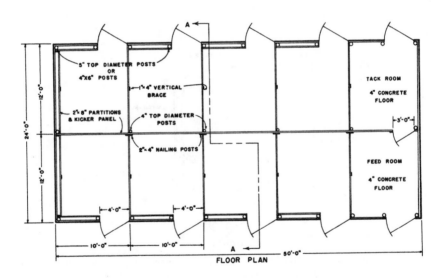

*Plan D-6010 developed by the Cooperative Plan Exchange, Beltsville, Maryland.

Fig. 125. Elevation and floor plan for D-6010.

The shed can be used in two ways. The first is to partition the shed into two conventional stalls as shown below. The second is to eliminate the partitions and leave the south or east side open. This will provide winter shelter which the horses can use free choice. It is adequate in most instances. Hay and/or grain storage can be provided in one end of the shed.

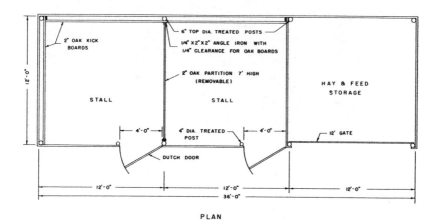

PLAN

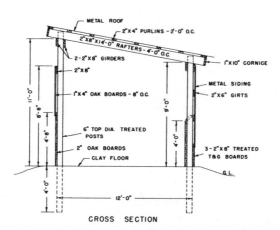

CROSS SECTION

Fig. 126. A double design, this shed can be left entirely open to provide shelter in cold weather where the land is bare of natural shelter features, or can be divided into two stalls and a feed/tack room, as shown, to become a small barn. Simplicity is the keynote, and pole construction makes for ease of building.

Fig. 127. (right) The good arrangement of a stall cannot be over-emphasized. Size is only one part, and while a stall may seem nothing more than a place for your horse to stand, it is much more and needs to be planned as such. Waterers, feed buckets, hay racks or bags, lighting, salt blocks, and ties all need to be carefully placed so that the stall can serve as anything from a spot to groom your horse in inclement weather to a small hospital in case of injury. This layout, from the Extension Division, Virginia Polytechnic Institute, Blacksburg, VA, is excellent.

STALL LAYOUT

One of the most important aspects of any horse barn is a stall arrangement that is convenient and safe for both the groom and his horse. The arrangement shown on this page fulfills these requirements; other arrangements, however, may be satisfactory. The essentials of the stall are: two screw eyes for cross-tying, screw eyes for a feed bucket and hay rack, an automatic waterer, and a salt and mineral block.

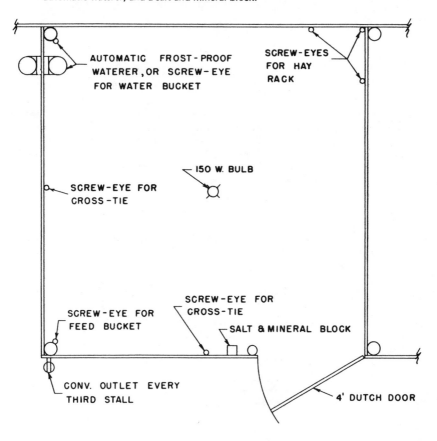

STALL   ARRANGEMENT

NOTES:
1. ALL SCREW-EYE BOLTS 1 5/8" RING DIA.
   2 3/4" LONG
2. A CUT-OFF VALVE MUST BE INSTALLED
   AT EACH WATERER TO PREVENT HOT
   HORSES FROM DRINKING TOO MUCH

do get a stallion, give him a bit more room, opening up the stall to at least fourteen by fourteen feet.

The stall is made so that there are no sharp protrusions, whether nails or board ends. Stall linings need to be at least four feet high, and should be of two-inch-thick oak boards, nailed horizontally. Ceiling height should be ten feet, and all

FEED ROOM

A feed room can be a pleasant, orderly room, or a cluttered, disorganized catchall. To avoid the latter, a workable arrangement of materials should be planned and maintained. The layout shown here has adequate tool storage for most barns, and the feed can be reached easily without moving any of the stored equipment.

Feed sacks are one of the main sources of clutter in a feed room. To relieve this problem, one sack can be hung by a corner, open end up, and then stuffed with all empty sacks until they are needed again.

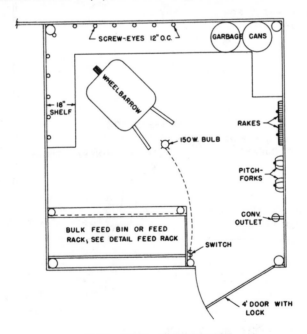

FEED ROOM ARRANGEMENT

Fig. 128. Feed rooms can be designed in many ways, but you'll note on this VPI arrangement the door opens outward, as discussed in the text, and there is plenty of room for storage of tools as well as feed.

A vermin-proof bin is a must in a feed room. The one shown in the detail is inexpensive and easy to construct. It offers an additional advantage in that bulk feed can be purchased and placed in the garbage can at the mill and then hauled to the barn at some savings in feed cost.

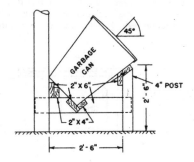

FEED RACK DETAIL

Fig. 129. A simple vermin-proof feed storage spot is made by tilting a galvanized metal—don't use plastic, as mice and other rodents will eat through most in a matter of minutes—against 2x4s set as shown.

doors should be eight feet tall (if they are to be used by the horse).

Stall sides must come right down to ground level: a stall with a few inches of space between its floor and the bottom stallboard can cause a horse to become cast when it tries to rise. That is, the horse can catch its feet or legs under the bottom of the board and be unable to rise. A cast horse will almost always panic and hurt itself, and may injure anyone coming in to try and assist.

Ventilation is important in all stalls, though a well-designed barn or stable will provide enough air circulation naturally to not need fans. Simply don't close the eave space under the rafters and your stable will have good air flow, assisted by any outside doors and windows. In extremely hot areas, you may find a need for fans at some times

Stable floors are often unfinished dirt in my area because the ground around here has a heavy clay content. In many other places, tamped clay is used, but if sufficient bedding is used, floors may be concrete or other materials.

TACK ROOM

Anyone who has purchased any riding equipment lately will testify to the value of good tack. In this respect, a well organized and maintained tack room is a good investment, because proper protection and cleaning of tack is essential to prolonging its useful life. Although all of the equipment shown in the arrangement on this page may not be necessary in all tack rooms, it certainly would be wise to leave space for it so that it can be added later. It would also be wise to put some insulation in the walls and ceiling of the tack room during construction, even if heating units are not immediately added.

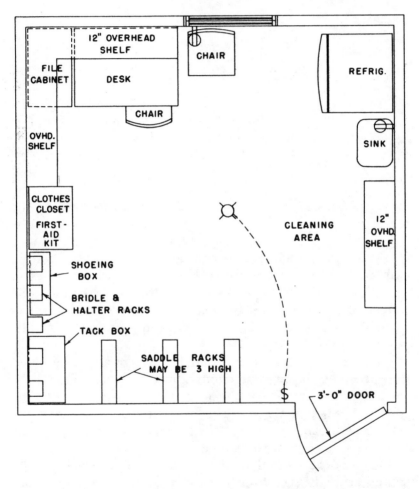

TACK ROOM ARRANGEMENT

Fig. 130. If you're to have a separate tack room—a nice feature if room is available—a design such as this might well be considered.

Grade around the barn or stable so that water runs away from the building, keeping the stalls at least eight inches above surrounding grade levels.

Lighting is provided by electricity, and is more or less essential to the modern stable. The equivalent of a single 100-watt incandescent bulb per stall is usually sufficient (you might also use a 40-watt florescent unit). Putting translucent fiberglass or other plastic panels in the roof is becoming more and more popular, but they do tend to cause a rise in summer stall temperatures.

Waterers of the automatic kind are fairly expensive for larger operations, but for the person who owns only a couple of horses, the overall cost isn't too bad. These should be heated, and the piping should be well below frost level for your area. If you prefer to hand carry water, use one of the heavy-duty plastic or rubber buckets available today. Don't use light plastic buckets as their durability is ridiculously poor, and metal buckets should also be avoided, for a horse stepping into one may bend it enough to form sharp, cutting edges.

The stable should open out onto a paddock, or onto the pasture.

Bedding for your horse is of great importance, and, today, makes up a goodly portion of the cost of keeping horses. It used to be that most woodworking places, sawmills, and other businesses were delighted to have horsemen pick up sawdust or wood chips and cart them away. Not anymore. In most areas, you'll have to pay for these items, with prices running as high as three dollars for a pick-up load, which is just about enough to do two stalls. Straw can also be used, but even that has risen to nearly a dollar a bale today.

Because of these rising costs, keeping the bedding as clean as possible is a big help in keeping stabling costs down. In other words, go in daily when your horse is stabled and use a manure fork and wheelbarrow or manure bucket to clear out the stall before you get a huge build-up that causes the bedding to need changing too often.

Feed storage can be something of a problem in a small stable, but the best solution is simply to build a separate feed room, with a concrete floor (place a drain in the floor, with a

SADDLE RACK NUMBER 1

A strong, yet collapsible, saddle rack is a handy convenience for horse shows. It allows you to keep your tack in good condition, even under the adverse circumstances of a show. The one pictured below is simple, yet adequate, for use both in the tack room and at shows.

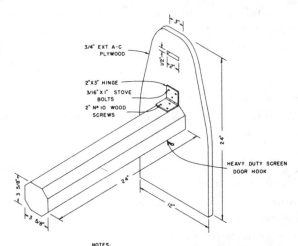

NOTES:
1. OCTAGONAL 4 X 4 TO BE COVERED WITH FLOOR CARPETING
2. AN EYE BOLT FASTENED TO THE WALL FITS THROUGH THE 1/2" X 2" SLOT TO HOLD THE RACK TO THE WALL.

SADDLE RACKS NUMBERS 2 AND 3

These saddle racks are somewhat sturdier than the collapsible one. They are also more adaptable to finishing, which will give the tack room a more pleasing appearance. When constructing a rack, be sure to do a good job of fastening the pieces together, since considerable pressure is exerted on the rack.

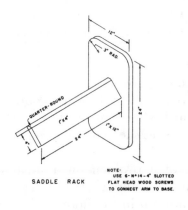

SADDLE RACK

NOTE:
USE 6-N°14-4" SLOTTED
FLAT HEAD WOOD SCREWS
TO CONNECT ARM TO BASE.

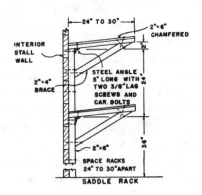

SADDLE RACK

dry well under it, and have the floor graded to the drain). Build sturdy feed bins, or use galvanized metal cans. Any feed bins built should be metal lined to keep rodents out, and should have tight-fitting tops. The feed room should have a sturdy door with a lock. The lock need not be elaborate, but it should be strong enough to prevent a horse from entering the feed room. For the same reason, the feed-room door should be attached so that it swings outward. Horses are sometimes too

SADDLE RACK NUMBER 4

One of the most convenient and least expensive types of saddle racks can be built from a 6" diameter cedar post. When not needed, the rack can be hooked to hang vertically. The rack can also be used for shows if a screw eye is provided. (A hexagonal post may be more desirable.) This portable rack works well when setting up your tack room at shows, etc.

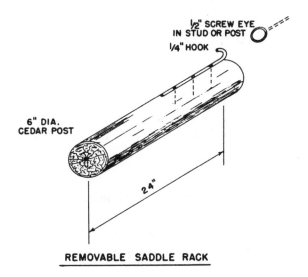

REMOVABLE SADDLE RACK

BRIDLE RACK NUMBER 1

A unique idea for a bridle rack is shown below. An old horse shoe, some horse shoe nails, three long wood screws to attach the rack to the wall, and a block of wood are the only materials required.

Figs. 131, 132 (left), and 133 (above). These are various types of easily built saddle racks, something that should be used for ever saddle if you desire the greatest durability.

REMOVABLE SADDLE RACK

BRIDLE RACK NUMBER 1

A unique idea for a bridle rack is shown below. An old horse shoe, some horse shoe nails, three long wood screws to attach the rack to the wall, and a block of wood are the only materials required.

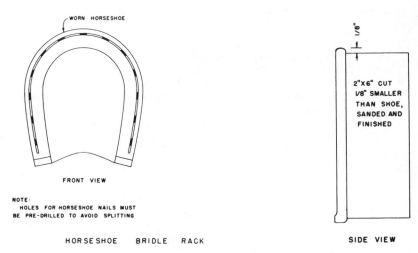

WORN HORSESHOE

FRONT VIEW

NOTE:
HOLES FOR HORSESHOE NAILS MUST
BE PRE-DRILLED TO AVOID SPLITTING

HORSESHOE   BRIDLE   RACK

1/8"

2"x6" CUT
1/8" SMALLER
THAN SHOE,
SANDED AND
FINISHED

SIDE VIEW

Fig. 134. A simple bridle rack, with building time of about 15 minutes. Most of that will be spent shaping the wood block with a jigsaw.

smart for their own good, and an inward-swinging door is easily burst open when a 1,110-pound equine backs its rump into it. At which time, should a feed bin have been left open, you've got major problems on your hand, for almost any horse will then eat itself into founder.

A separate tack room is a nice touch, too. It need not be as large as the feed room, but the door needs to be as sturdy, for a curious horse nosing about amongst saddles and such can do an awful lot of damage.

Good locks on tack-room doors are a tremendous help in other ways. In the past four years, a friend of mine has had two Western saddles stolen from his tack room, one of them an irreplaceable Porter he had ridden and loved for years. Tack is

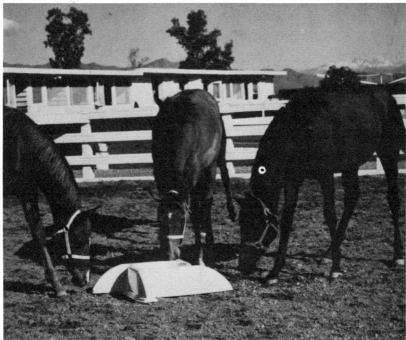

Fig. 134A. One of Farnam's ground level feeders. Credit: Farnam Companies.

relatively expensive, so locking it up securely is a simple and smart precaution.

Simple sheds can be used for shelter in reasonably mild areas where there is little other shelter from winds. Depending on locale, and prevailing winds, you would usually leave the east or south sides open.

Fig. 134B. A corner style hay rack from Farnam. Credit: Farnam Companies.

Fig. 134C. Set up inside or outside, this hay rack is large enough to handle two or three horses easily. Credit: Farnam Companies.

Fig. 134D. A prefab barn, available from Farnam Companies. Credit: Farnam Companies.

Fig. 134E. Prefab interiors are attractive and strong. Credit: Farnam Companies.

On pages 187—200 are some small barn design patterns, which are simply floor layouts. If you take the numbers from the one you find best suits your needs, your state extension division will usually provide plans at low cost. The stall-layout pattern gives an indication of good stall layout for a convenient and safe set-up. Two easy-to-build saddle rack drawings are also here; with the cheapest commercial saddle rack going for about eighteen dollars, these can save a bit of expense.

To make a bridle-cleaning rack, simply pick up about four horseshoes, new or used as you wish, and a foot-long piece of rod with an eye in the end. Make sure the rod is steel, and either weld, or have someone else weld, the four horseshoes to the bottom of the rod. Insert a moderate-sized hook in a convenient beam or part of the ceiling and hook the bridle-cleaning rack on that. It's easily removed when cleaning is done, or can be left up as a bridle rack.

If a horse is fed either grain or hay as a supplement while on pasture, most people simply toss the feed down, or get some sort of upright feeder. The best bet is a ground-level feeder, for that's the horse's normal eating position. Not only that, ground-level feeding serves as a good weight reduction method for horses with fat necks. Several are available, with the one shown coming from Farnam Companies, or you can make your own out of heavy wood.

Hay racks for stalls should be ample, and are a bit of a pain to build properly and strongly enough to really last. Commercial models are neater looking and less likely to have protruding edges.

If you don't believe in doing it yourself, or can't, prefabricated barns are easily found, and prefab interiors for just about any barn are also available in several forms. For that matter, you can also buy easily set-up and taken-down corrals and stalls for those horse shows where you'll be staying quite a few days.

Fig. 134F. Exterior, portable corrals, barns, and paddocks are readily available. Credit: Farnam Companies.

If you want it for your horse today, you can almost certainly find it, either in the form of plans from your local extension agent or in the form of commercially made products from a number of sources. The choice of do-it-yourself comes down to one between you and your wallet most of the time, though in some cases you are going to have to buy and not make—I don't remember the last time I saw anyone actually capable of making a wooden bucket, though it is possible. The many heavy-duty plastic items on the market can make life easier for both horse and horse owner these days.

9. PARASITES AND FIRST AID

At one time or another, every horse is going to need some sort of minor or major first aid, and at all times a good, comprehensive worming program is necessary. Worms are the bane of the domesticated horse's existence, and must be controlled if the animal is to be healthy.

Shell Chemical Company calls worming the horse internal grooming, and, with the proper worming medicine, that's probably a good term as it indicates the horse is as clean inside as it is out.

Mixed among the nastier effects of the various worms a horse is likely to pick up are overall anemia and the loss of nutrition in general, so that overall condition may drop off badly in a short period of time. Shell's Dr. T. J. Fogg states unequivocally that "there is no such thing as a worm-free horse," as do many other veterinarians. Parasitology has recently developed well beyond the old farmer's method of mixing some tobacco or tobacco juice in the animal's feed, and the overall health of our horses has improved as a result.

Until recently, most people seemed to feel that worming a couple of times a year—right after the first frost and sometime early in summer or late in spring—was sufficient, but recent tests have shown that some kinds of parasites can reinfect your horse in as little as three weeks. What are these nasty little things? Well, there are four common internal parasites that you and your horse need worry about.

Bots, or gastrophilus, are the eggs of the adult botfly and are found from late summer through fall on the hair of your horse's legs, neck, and head, and in heavy infestations, as I've seen recently, right up to the belly and the barrel. The horse will lick or nip at these eggs; the moist heat of the mouth causes them to hatch. These larvae then migrate through the tissues of the mouth, emerge into the mouth or throat and are swallowed, moving on to the stomach. The larvae then attach themselves to the stomach lining and grow through the winter. Larvae pass into the fecal matter during the spring and become the mature botfly. Damage is done to the stomach lining; in extreme cases rupture of the stomach may result. Interference with digestion is high. As suggested earlier, washing the legs with warm water causes the eggs to hatch externally, after which they can be washed away. Bot knives and razors are also used to reduce the infestation.

E. INCIDENCE OF WORMS BY SEASONS:

(429 Horses From Kentucky, Illinois, Indiana, Ohio, Wisconsin, Texas, Arizona, New Mexico, Oklahoma, Colorado.)

	SPRING	SUMMER	FALL	WINTER
BOTS	√√√	√√	√√	√√√
ASCARID	√√	√√√	√√	√
STRONGYLUS V	√	√	√√	√√√
STRONGYLUS E + E	√√√	√	√	√√√
SMALL STRONGYLUS	√√	√√√	√√√	√√√

√ = Moderate Incidence
√√ = High Incidence
√√√ = Very High Incidence

Fig. 135. Worm incidence chart.

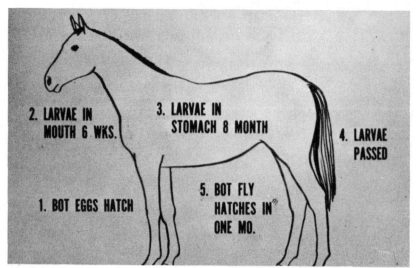

Fig. 136. Life cycle of bots.

Pinworms, or oxyuris, are found, as adult worms, in the rear intestinal tract close to the rectum and anus. Females move to the anus and deposit their eggs around the opening. Eggs are then dropped to stall bedding, onto pasture, into the feed and water in general, and are eventually eaten by the horse. The eggs develop into larvae in the large intestine, and do not migrate from there. Primary damage is from irritation causing the horse to become a tail rubber.

Strongyles, or bloodworms, start as eggs on pasture, where they take about seven days to develop to the infective stage—a female strongyle may lay as many as 5,000 eggs in a single day.

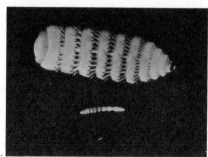

Fig. 137. Bots.

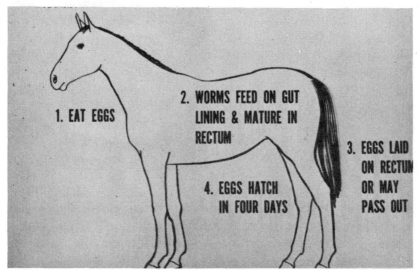

Fig. 138. Pinworm life cycle.

The larvae are picked up as the horse feeds, from whence they enter the intestinal tract and penetrate the wall of the intestine. The migration continues up the blood vessels, causing damage and irritation as the movement continues. Reduced blood flow to the intestine may result, so the horse becomes colicky, but

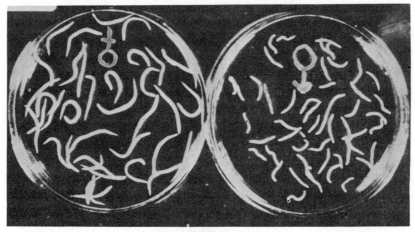

Fig. 139. Pinworms.

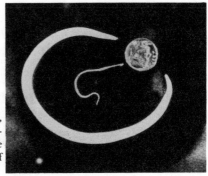

Fig. 140. Comparative worm sizes, though many are much smaller (of different kinds than these) and many are much larger (again, different breeds of worms).

other damage may also be caused, including damage to the heart, liver, and the lining of the abdominal cavity. The larvae cannot be treated by wormers until they reenter the intestinal tract, where they come as adults, attaching themselves to the walls, sucking blood, and producing eggs.

Roundworms, ascarids, are the hardiest of all equine parasites, since neither heat nor cold does much to damage them, and their dormant span may extend for many months. The adults in the upper intestine lay eggs, while interfering with

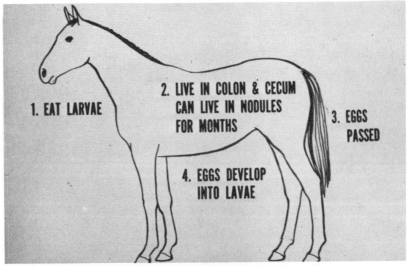

1. EAT LARVAE

2. LIVE IN COLON & CECUM CAN LIVE IN NODULES FOR MONTHS

3. EGGS PASSED

4. EGGS DEVELOP INTO LAVAE

Fig. 141. Life cycle of small bloodworms (strongyles).

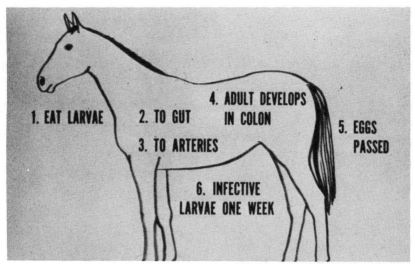

Fig. 142. Life cycle of large bloodworms (strongyles).

digestion, causing a hyperactivity of the tract—with one of the milder results being severe diarrhea—and may, with very heavy infestation, block the entire intestine, rupturing it and killing the horse. Eggs pass onto the ground in manure, the horse ingests the eggs and the larvae, which then hatch in the intes-

AGE	PERCENTAGE
FOALS	58%
YEARLINGS	37%
2 YRS.	20%
3 YRS.	20%
4 YRS. & OLDER	10%

Fig. 143. Roundworm infection rate.

tine. Migrating roundworms move to the liver, causing renal damage, and move to the lungs, resulting often in a dry, hacking cough. The larvae brought up during the coughing are swallowed, and move then to the upper intestine, where they develop into adults.

A real series of horror stories, isn't it? Nevertheless, a good worming program, with a series of effective wormers, will prevent just about all the damage mentioned and, in combination with good sanitation methods, will help keep reinfestation to a minimum. But there is no stopping. Worming programs must be started at a young age and continued for the life of the horse. Today there are at least nine chemicals or chemical combinations used as wormers. It is recommended by practically all equine experts that you switch from one to another at certain intervals so that the parasites in your animals don't get a chance to build up their own immune reaction to the worming medicines, as will certainly happen if the same wormer is used all the time.

A basic worming program starts with treatment at two months of age and is continued on a year-round basis. A broad

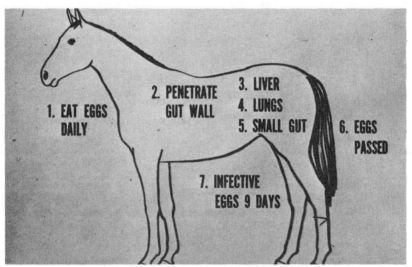

Fig. 144. Life cycle of large roundworms.

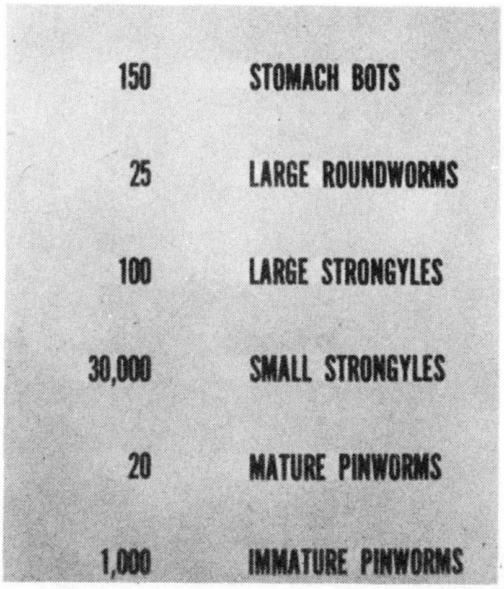

150	STOMACH BOTS
25	LARGE ROUNDWORMS
100	LARGE STRONGYLES
30,000	SMALL STRONGYLES
20	MATURE PINWORMS
1,000	IMMATURE PINWORMS

Fig. 145. An average parasite load for a grade horse is shown here.

spectrum wormer, killing most types of the worms we've mentioned, is used. (The life cycles covered above are for the basic parasites: bloodworms come in three basic varieties with offshoots of those.) Treatment should be made at shorter than previously considered intervals (consider that a bloodworm may reach ten inches in length in less than three months, and you can see how ineffective twice-yearly worming may be). Actual worming dates may vary. If you have a single horse on a large pasture, you may go ten or even twelve weeks without worming, but if you have that same horse confined to a small paddock you may need to worm about every six to eight weeks. In cases of severe crowding, and in cases where infestation in the past has been extremely heavy, monthly worming may be best.

Before worming any horse, the best procedure is to take a fecal sample to your veterinarian for analysis of worm content. Indiscriminate worming is better than no worming, but is a waste in several ways (it costs about six dollars, or did recently, for enough Shell's Dichlorvos wormer for a 900-pound horse, so if you need worming only every 90 days, you save money over monthly worming: tube worming by your vet will be more expensive, but may be more effective, especially if infestation is

Fig. 146. Get rid of the parasite load, and the result will be healthy horses. Of course, getting rid of the total load is, today, impossible, but correct treatment keeps the number of parasites below the level where they cause major harm.

heavy or if the horse is ill in some other way—most wormers should not be used on horses that are ill or in poor condition).

Wormers come in different forms, as already indicated. Some pastes are squirted by the owner into the horse's mouth—some horses object strongly to this, while others are hardly bothered. You may have to have a vet tube worm a horse that picks out granules of feed-mix wormers and refuses to accept a gel in its mouth. Many people prefer tube worming in any case, as it tends to get more of the active wormer into the stomach, but such worming for a noncommercial horseman, on a regular basis, can get a bit expensive.

The different wormers available today will provide nearly complete protection if used as recommended (make sure you read the wormer label to find out just which chemical you're getting). As we mentioned, switch off wormers, using at least two different kinds, and preferably three, over the course of a year.

Wormer   Removal of –%:

	Bots	Round-worms	Strongyles	Pinworms
Thiabendazole	0	10-30	90-100	90-100
Dichlorvos	80-100	95-100	70-100	90-100
Pyrantel	0	90-100	70-100	60-70
Thiabendazole + Piperazine	0	95-100	95-100	30-40
Piperazine	0	95-100	10-60	50-70
Phenothiazine + Piperazine + Carbon Disulfide	78-85	95-100	95-100	50-70
Phenothiazine + Piperazine	0	95-100	90-100	50-70
Piperazine + Carbon Disulfide	78-85	95-100	40-60	40-60
Trichlorfon	90-100	95-100	0-10	90-100

As you can see, there is nothing that is, as yet, an absolutely perfect wormer, but a few come close. You may have to drop from your ideal wormer once or twice a year to keep the bugs from getting used to it, but in general there is little or no excuse for an extreme infestation of worms of any kind in the modern horse if the owner will only do his job.

There are precautions with each and every wormer used, and a few should probably be listed, even though the containers should also have the listing. Piperazine is not for use with horses in poor condition, and overdose symptoms for other horses include a loss of coordination and diarrhea. Dichlorvos is not safe for very young foals nor mares in late pregnancy, and should never be used with insecticides, tranquilizers, or stimulants. Overdose symptoms are colic and incoordination. Trichlorfon is not safe for mares in late pregnancy and an overdose will show up in the form of colic, loss of coordination, and diarrhea. Phenothiazine is used in a low-level daily dose, for single large doses will make your horse dull and weak, bring on colic and a fever, constipation, and a rapid pulse. Thiabendazole is not for use with horses in poor condition, and overdosing can bring on colic and depression.

In other words, make sure your horse is in at least reasonable condition, and then use only the recommended dose for the animal's body weight. Dichlorvos is probably the most effective wormer, but it is extremely powerful and label precautions *must* be adhered to, right up to keeping the horse away from any pest-killing strip for a couple of hours after worming.

There are one or two other chemical wormer combinations on the market, but those listed are the most popular and any two should provide an effective worming program, and a safe one if used as directed. If you have any doubts about the condition of your horse, or your ability to judge amounts, then it's best to have your vet at least start off your worming program and lay out the rest of it for you.

A quick check of the above table will show that about 98 percent of all horses, East and West, were found to be infected with bloodworms, while a look through the other forms of worms will show that infestation was, for all practical purposes, 100 percent. Checking further with the age table, we come up with the same figures. All of this demands an effective worming program on the part of today's horseman.

FIRST AID

Horses are like humans in that they get a wide range of bangs, sprains, scrapes, bruises, and cuts. This means a few items are necessary in the equine medicine chest, and a knowledge of how to use those items is also more than just helpful. I don't intend to go into a wide variety of equine diseases in this section, for I'm not a veterinarian; your vet should check your horse's records for any necessary local immunizations, particularly tetanus, and give what shots are needed. Most horse owners are wise to refrain from trying to do too much of the work that a vet does, for there are techniques and a great deal of specialized knowledge involved in much of the work. It's possible to clean and bandage wounds and to give intramuscular shots (with practice), to give the horse aid and comfort while awaiting the vet, and to work to eliminate symptoms of fungi and such.

Still, in some cases you're much wiser to leave treatment of even seemingly simple things to a vet, or a vet and farrier. Hoof cracks are one area the average horse owner shouldn't fool with, as are puncture wounds of the hoof and other areas.

When considering first aid for the variety of cuts and abrasions your horse may receive, remember that the horse has very thin skin, and that wounds below the knees and hocks are especially hard to handle and sensitive because of the lack of muscle under the skin. Careful treatment will often include the use of bandages in such areas.

A good wound dressing or powder is an essential for every horse owner. This powder or dressing needs four main qualities: it must help stop bleeding; it must kill germs; it must dry the wound to discourage flies from laying eggs in the cut; it must discourage the growth of proud flesh.

Proud flesh is granulated tissue in extreme amounts, so much so that it fills in the wound above the original area of skin. Should such granulation occur, you'll have to remove excessive amounts (generally, anything over a quarter of an inch above the skin surface is considered excessive enough for removal). You can snip this off with a pair of sterile scissors, or call your vet to do the job. For most of us, calling the vet is the best solution.

Proud flesh generally results from excessive moisture and slow healing. Generally, a wound should be washed with a mild surgical soap only once. After that, it is kept dry and, if necessary, bandaged. No wound that requires stitching should be washed unless your vet specifically tells you to do so.

Contents of the equine first-aid kit will vary a bit from area to area, and from horseman to horseman, but some items are standard. If you don't wish to give your horse shots, then you will not need syringes (many more horsemen are giving their own shots these days—intramuscular only—and the process is not all that difficult in most cases, and with most horses).

A good starting point for any equine first-aid kit is a mild surgical soap. Add a batt of cotton or some cotton balls for washing wounds, as most cloths are too harsh. An antibiotic eye ointment is necessary, as is a repellent cream to keep insects away from open wounds. Nitrofurazone powder is good for general use on wounds that aren't to be bandaged, while the salve is applied to wounds that are bandaged. A mildly antiseptic jelly or cream is good for use on superficial scrapes. A thrush ointment or paste should be kept on hand. Some of the thrush treatments are also excellent for use on small wounds at or near the hoof coronet.

Add a couple of rolls of inch-wide adhesive and several elastic bandages, four and six inches wide. Also a box or two of sterile gauze pads, three inches square, will prove handy, as will sheet cotton or other padding to use under bandages.

I've found that the various 3M brands of dressings and tapes are excellent, and their pressure-sensitive, self-adhering foam pads and rolls are also fine. Their Vetrap brand of bandaging tape seems to be the brand of choice in my area and in several others.

Pick up a pair of bandage scissors (those are the bent-nosed kind carried by almost all nurses) and a small pair of curved-point scissors for trimming hair around wounds not needing sutures.

Fig. 147. 3M Company's bandages are excellent, but these self-adhering foam wraps can sometimes be even better. The nonallergenic tape is also fine. The clear eyes ointment is from Farnam, as is the Superhoof spray. (Author's photo.)

A mild liniment is useful for minor muscle soreness from overexertion and fatigue. Diluted liniment is a good bracer to use after a horse has been worked hard, but generally it is applied full strength to the affected part, with vigorous rubbing for about five minutes. Use the liniment you select according to the manufacturer's directions, and as your vet directs.

Disinfectants are, strictly speaking, not a part of your first-aid kit, but are needed many times to break bacterial cycles so that healing can take place. Any disinfectants used on the horse itself should be of the mildest type available, such as boric acid, though that is now being replaced by saline solutions and antibiotic solutions. Check with your veterinarian for his recommendations. Saline solutions, by the way, are *not* salt water or brine types, but very mild solutions that cause little or no irritation when properly applied.

Alcohol is primarily a skin disinfectant and is sometimes used for disinfecting surgical instruments if you are in a hurry.

Chlorine disinfectants (probably the best known are Clorox and Purex bleaches) knock off just about every type of bacteria and fungi, but they will corrode many metals, and are not for use on skin.

Iodine is a useful skin disinfectant and may aid healing or minor cuts and abrasions. It is probably more easily applied to horses if you use a twitch, as it tends to sting badly (it is actually the alcohol in the tincture that causes the stinging). Tamed iodine is much more expensive, but is almost as effective as iodine, without the sting, though any wounds so treated must be thoroughly cleaned before use.

Phenols such as carbolic acid have been in use many years and are still among the cheapest and most effective general disinfectants you can find. Unfortunately, phenols are toxic to both humans and horses, so care is needed in their use; follow the manufacturer's directions explicitly.

The treatment of wounds follows a series of steps, which in turn depend on the severity of the wound. In the case of really severe wounds, stop at step number two, while you can continue on past that with less severe wounds, in fact, often dropping step two.

Step one is a simple one that may require complex measures. Your first job is to stop the bleeding. In most cases, a simple pressure bandage will do the job, but if a large artery or vein is severed, you may need to use a tourniquet. There are rules for the use of a tourniquet, and, if used improperly, the device can cause a lot of damage, whether the subject is human or equine. First, the tourniquet goes between the cut member and the heart. It is tightened only until blood flow stops. It is released for at least ten minutes out of every half hour (in other words, wait twenty minutes, then back it off and let the blood flow to the animal's extremities, so that tissue damage and possible necrosis can't result). It can then be retightened. In any wound where you need a tourniquet, your immediate next step after blood flow stops, is step two: call your veterinarian. The call to the vet as step two applies in any case of really severe bleeding, even if pressure bandaging stops the flow, and it also applies in cases of larger surface cuts where you think suturing may be needed.

Step three is cleaning the wound. Unless your vet tells you otherwise on wounds needing suturing, leave this step to him. If the wound is small, wash it with a mild soap or a saline solution, removing all foreign material such as gravel, sand, etc. Torn tissue, if loose, is also removed.

For step four, clip or shave long hair, trying to get an overall length of about half an inch or just a bit less.

Using a small ear syringe, apply first-aid powder as the manufacturer directs on the label. After step five, have your vet check the wound to see if suturing may be needed. Of course, for obviously large wounds your vet would already be there and your work would have stopped at step two. This, though, is a vet's decision, and can be a moot question on some wounds. Leave it to your vet.

Step seven involves tetanus protection. Check the shot records for your horse to see if it needs the antitoxin (used if the horse is not already immunized), or a toxoid booster.

Step eight comes a few days later as the wound starts to form a scab. At this time, you should change from first-aid powder to first-aid salve. Large wounds require a vet's inspection before making the change, as the too-moist large wound will almost certainly form proud flesh, causing large scab formation and slow healing if ointment or salve is used too soon.

A salve used on a wound that is still open, and unbandaged, can easily pick up dirt and debris and thus become infected.

The use of antibiotics for wound treatment is left up to the veterinarian.

Most veterinarians now recommend against the use of caustics to treat abrasions and other cuts on the horse because of the resulting tissue damage.

If the wound is a bad one, a further step is needed. The horse is placed in a clean stall to restrict movement that might tear out sutures or otherwise cause the wound to reopen.

The restraint of your horse during treatment will often depend on the severity of the wound. For really bad cuts, it may be nearly impossible to handle the animal without major restraints, whether tranquilizers or a twitch. For smaller wounds, cross tying is often effective. The vet will be the one to decide about tranquilizers, of course, but before he comes in you may have to decide on the use of a twitch.

A twitch is usually a device with a handle between one and two feet long, with a foot-long rope or chain on one end, formed in a loop. It is applied over the upper lip, making sure the nasal cartilage is not caught. Twist the twitch so the lip is pinched. The resulting pain will take the animal's mind off even a bad wound and allow you to treat it.

While the twitch sounds cruel, it is sometimes the only possible way to get a horse to stand quietly while a wound is treated. Properly used, it causes no permanent damage (never use a twitch on an ear!). Don't stand in front of the horse, either.

Giving intramuscular injections can be a risky business for the horse owner and for that reason is still often left to the vet. In no case should you be the one, anyway, to diagnose the reasons for the injection: that must be done by someone who has qualified for the job, and that someone is your veterinarian. And, no matter how clear my explanation of giving an IM injection may sound, do not attempt to give the first few yourself without the instruction, and presence, of your vet. The vet can instruct you in needle sizes for the various fluids to be injected and can provide assistance in mastering details of the process.

The IM injection begins with syringe preparation. Today, almost everyone uses disposable syringes, cutting down on the worries about needle sterility (never, ever reuse the needle on a disposable syringe). First, break the seal on the syringe container and slide the syringe needle out, making sure you touch only the plunger end. If you accidentally touch the needle, it must either be resterilized or discarded.

Fill the syringe with air to the same amount of medicine you'll need (two cc. of medicine requires you to draw the plunger back to the two cc. mark). Place the bottle of medicine in your left hand, keeping it tilted so that the air is at the top of the bottle. If the protective seal on the bottle is still in place, remove that and wipe the top of the bottle with alcohol. Slip the syringe through the seal at about a 45-degree downward angle, pulling the bottle up onto the needle and keeping the needle in the airspace at the top of the bottle.

Tilt the bottle upward to place the tip of the needle in the medicine and push the plunger forward to expel part of the air (about two cc. at a time at the most). Pull the plunger back to draw in some fluid, and repeat the process until you have removed the needed amount of medicine. Keep the bottle up and tap the barrel of the syringe so it will expend any air bubbles back into the bottle. Slip the needle carefully out of the bottle, making sure you do not jar the plunger and lose some of the dose. Place the syringe cap back on the needle until it is time to actually give the shot.

The actual procedure of giving the shot starts with restraining the horse. Depending on the animal, you will need someone holding a lead rope from the halter or cross ties. Some horses are so calm about properly given shots, they need almost no restraint, while others tend to get a bit panicky if they even imagine a shot is coming.

The syringe is held in the hand to be used to give the injection, and that hand is gently laid on the neck, knuckles first, with the needle pointed a bit away from the neck. The heel of the hand or the knuckles are used to gently tap the neck a few times to get the horse used to pressure in the area. It is best to use the same motion and just about the same force, or a hair more, as you will require for giving the injection. On the fourth or fifth rise of the hand, the syringe is turned so the needle is pointed at the injection site and is then passed through the skin with the same motion and force as before. Keep the heel of the hand, or your forearm, in contact with your animal's neck as you insert the needle so you can stay with the horse should it shy.

Wait for the horse to calm down before proceeding. Turn the volume scale on the syringe toward you, and look to see if blood is coming back into the medicine. If so, you've hit a blood vessel and must repeat the process of inserting the needle. If not, and if the horse has calmed and is standing well, slowly and steadily inject the medication. Hold the syringe between your first two fingers and use your thumb to push down the plunger.

Withdraw the needle slowly and steadily, and then use your hand to rub the site for a minute or so to help further calm the horse.

In cases where you get a large volume of blood in the syringe after needle insertion, or any other substance, it is much wiser to back off and call your vet, so he can check to see what you're doing wrong, or what may be wrong with your horse.

Keep an eye on your horse for a few minutes. Probably 90 percent of any adverse reactions will develop within the first ten minutes of injection. Obviously, you should call your vet if you notice any signs of strange behavior.

Destroy the needle and syringe once they're used.

The neck site is not the only spot where horses are injected, of course, but is used as an example. Depending on need, and your vet's advice, injections may also be given in the rump, shoulder, or hindquarters.

Not everyone, probably not even most of you, will wish to give IM injections, but for the few, the previous is an outline, and an outline only. Your veterinarian must supervise the first shots you give and will explain how to handle any problems that may crop up.

Some experts say that tying a horse before giving an injection is a bad idea, but I feel that a horse that is cross tied when you're working alone is much easier to handle. Simply trying to get the horse to hold still for an injection with nothing providing any sort of restraint can present problems in many cases. Tying may make a skittish horse more nervous, but it is up to you to get your horse used to such methods, possibly using them for grooming of kinds your horse particularly prefers even though restraint then is absolutely unneeded (most horses of my acquaintance will accept certain forms of grooming—light currying, brushing, etc.—with no restraint whatsoever, with your biggest problem being keeping the horse from leaning against you to make you brush or curry a bit harder). If the horse associates the tying with a form of pleasure, it will become less nervous. For this reason, it probably will also pay you to spend some time grooming a horse after giving it an injection.

As you'll note throughout this treatise on first aid and parasitology, I keep recommending you call your veterinarian. Too many horse owners seem to set up an adversary relationship with their vets, calling them only when things have gotten so extreme the vet has to take drastic measures to save the horse, thus costing huge amounts of money and possibly losing the animal anyway. Which tends to lead to a stronger adversary relationship, or cause you to change vets altogether.

One of the most important factors in horse care is the selection and cultivation of a good veterinarian who works extensively with large animals. Cat and dog doctors often tend to stick with those animals, so they may, or may not, be suitable for your horse's needs. If a vet doesn't care to work with equines, he should tell you right away.

A check with your extension agent will usually get a list of good, local large-animal veterinarians. Checking with other horse owners is a help, but not always a great help, as personality clashes have a way of entering into the vet/owner relationship as in any other.

The job is basically up to you. Some tips may help. First, if the vet appears extremely nervous around your horse and wants the animal heavily restrained or sedated even for a tube worming, when you know your horse will put up little, if any, resistance, forget it. Move on to another vet. More obvious is the vet who simply doesn't like horses. He'll work with them, but doesn't much care for the animals.

Generally, consideration for you and your horse should be a part of the veterinarian's stock in trade. If he's to be at your place Monday at 8 A.M., and shows up Wednesday with no call to you, ride on to the next. Emergencies can, and frequently do, happen in veterinary practice, but if the vet misses his assigned time and day, you should at least be informed that he'll be late, or receive a later call explaining the situation.

Veterinary doctors are good and bad, just as are human doctors. Remember that, in both cases, half these people finished in the bottom halves of their classes. But also remember that classroom work isn't everything. Empathy is a lot, and with the state of equine medical and other research, that can be most of it.

Whatever the case, check out two or three veterinarians first before settling on the one you consider the best. And then rely on him (or her). Keep in touch whenever you have problems that require his assistance, advice, or outright care, and don't wait until your horse is down in its stall and unable to eat or get up. The resuts will be worthwhile, for you'll have a healthier horse and more peace of mind.

10. HORSE SAFETY

In one sense, this book has emphasized safety all the way through, but in another there are some special problems and needs that need either emphasis, or reemphasis, now. Much of safety on a horse is related to common sense, about which I tend to agree with Mark Twain. Common sense is not a good name for it, simply because a solid dose is so uncommon.

A few days ago, I had an experience with a skittish horse that serves to illustrate. The animal is relatively small, about 14-1, and has been poorly trained in general. It is seldom ridden (about once every eight weeks, I think), and tends to be very stubborn. The horse started out after another as I was mounting. I checked him—four times. This was after considerable trouble bitting him and saddling him. I finally mounted a standing horse, which immediately broke into a canter with no cues. No response to the reins. Finally, hard leg cues and reining harder than I like turned the animal. Then he bucked.

Two minutes later, that horse was standing there without a saddle or a rider. The day was windy, the woods noisy, he was stubborn and skittish. And I was in no mood to get thrown on my knee-surgery scars. The horse won, but is badly in need of basic training so I didn't worry about that training factor— generally it's not a good idea to let the animal know it is capable of winning. Common sense said my trail ride was more likely to turn into a rodeo, which I simply didn't want. So I got off and will await a calmer day.

Safety starts with selecting the correct horse for you, as mentioned earlier. It also starts with spending your first few saddle hours with a capable instructor, no matter how gentle your horse is.

From this point, we move on to more general items. The stable area should be as fireproof as possible, with easily acces- should be discarded or stored elsewhere. Bedding wastes should be treated the same way, and flammable items such as gasoline or fuel for tractors and such should be stored elsewhere.

In the tack room, keep your oily rags to a minimum and string them on a line instead of heaping them in a pile in a corner.

Watch your smoking habits closely around any stable area. Better still, don't smoke in such areas.

Keep any poisons out of reach of horses and children.

Use the stall dimensions as shown in the chapter on stables.

Use safe fencing, not barbed wire or one-sided fencing (one-sided fencing is actually alright, if the boards are attached from the side on which a horse might be expected to impact them).

Don't halter a pastured horse.

Clear pastures of debris, unsafe structures, and crotched trees.

Keep an eye on tack condition and repair or replace any items showing excessive wear.

Handle your horse with a reasonable amount of caution, even though he is an animal of flight rather than fight. Don't run up to horses, especially from their blind sides. Walk slowly and calmly to the horse, speaking in a calm tone of voice.

Avoid clattering and crashing noises around horses that are to be handled any time soon.

Use your knowledge of your horse to check on his moods as you approach him. Horses have their off days just as we do, and we'll be well repaid for not getting upset about them.

Don't tease your horse, or anyone's horse.

Remember that your horse is likely to think you're the same size and weight he is. Your eyes are on a level, possibly even higher, than the animal's, and his brain may well be interpreting your size, thus, as equal to or greater than his. Horses can thus rub against you, slamming you into the stall side, and so on. I've had this happen, simply because the horse was friendly and I was careless, at a time when I already had four broken ribs and a cracked sternum. There is no way to describe the feeling.

Watch that gentle, sleepy horse as you approach him. Do your best to come up from the side, making sure he knows you're around. Startle the gentlest horse and it's likely to kick and kick hard.

Don't grab at any horse's head. This often seems the hardest thing for young children to learn. Side vision magnifies the size of the approaching hand, and can badly startle a horse if much speed is used, while forward vision is just about nil, so a glance won't show your hand until it touches the muzzle, which will cause many horses to shy away or rear.

Keep your head and feet out of your horse's way. A horse can simply raise its head and do a fair job of giving you a concussion. Keeping your feet out from under his is a good idea for obvious reasons.

If you must walk behind a horse, up close, make sure he knows you're there by speaking and placing a hand on his rump as you approach his rear and sliding that hand along with firm, but not extreme, pressure. Stay in as close to the rump as possible, for then if the horse should kick, the power will be reduced. Keep an eye on the animal's reactions as you move around: should the horse decide to kick, give his rump a good shove and *stay in close.*

When entering a stall where a horse is loose, again make sure you let it know you're coming. The horse should be trained to turn to anyone coming in, and you should not enter until it does so.

Approaching a pastured horse has some of the same elements, should he be off in a corner of woods and drowsing a bit. Some horses will readily approach their owners, while others will need to be walked up to. Come up to your horse at a slight side angle so you're in his line of vision. If your horse is the kind who enjoys a bit of frolic with you before standing, either stay ouside the fence and let him finish playing or stand your ground inside the fence. Moving away from what seems to be a charge is likely to make the horse lose sight of you and may cause you to get run down. Most horses won't step on humans, or anything else soft and squishy, given a choice. If you don't know the horse, don't get in the pasture with him.

Always lead a horse from one side or the other, never from in front. Under no circumstances should you ever wrap a lead rope, or reins, around your hand or tie them to any part of your body or clothing. Even a small horse can give you a pretty bad dragging if it panics.

Follow safe saddling procedures: halter first, then saddle, then bit and headstall, with the halter around the neck. The front girth is tightened first and loosened last.

Mount with the reins held so they just check the horse, but not so they're tight enough to cause the horse to back.

It's safest to lead the horse a few steps after the girth is tightened and then recheck for tightness, in case your horse is a sweller.

Don't mount where there are overhead obstacles. Never mount indoors.

Keep a watch on your horse, paying special attention to the ears and to body attitude. You'll be able to see displeasure if ears flatten, and you can often spot the horse settling down to buck as you mount.

Generally, staying alert and making sure your horse is alert on the trail are safety features.

If the footing on a trail is bad, slow down. Dismount if it gets really bad, but don't lead your horse across streams or other areas where he might be in a rush to get across and run you down.

Learn to fall. Sooner or later just about everyone who rides a horse is going to fall or get thrown. Learning to fall in a ball instead of flat is a help in reducing the resulting aches and pains.

Riding along roads requires a few other precautions. First, make sure you can control your horse well before riding along roads with traffic. Then stay especially alert, for footing on pavement is not the best, and a car or motorcycle with a noisy muffler can startle even the most gentle horse. Road bridges, culverts, and other such obstacles may spook some horses. Usually it's best to ride such obstacles first with a more experienced horseman and horse leading so your horse will get a chance to become accustomed to the different feel and noise of such surfaces.

Dogs. I love dogs, but they are sometimes a pain when riding roadsides. Your horse must be accustomed to a dog who might snap at its heels. Some will even bite the horse, and this is almost guaranteed to produce an instant rodeo. Personally, I feel a rider who constantly has to pass a biting or nipping dog is justified in carrying a lunging whip and snapping it at the dog's back.

Children. Their curiosity can cause problems. Don't ride a horse on the streets where you can expect to see children unless he's unspookable by them.

Trail-riding safety was pretty heavily covered back a bit, so should need litte elaboration now. Simply look for obstacles and stay alert, after learning well both your and your animal's capacities.

Generally, the basic rules of courtesy will make for safe horse handling, with a few needed techniques added in. If you are courteous to other riders, and to nonhorsemen, and firm in your control of your horse, while still having consideration for its needs, then problems should be few and far between. Going too fast for your skills, or too fast for your horse's skills, though, will almost always get you into trouble.

Take your time learning and don't try to jump from the unskilled rider to top horseman in three months. Take your time in familiarizing yourself with your horse, letting him get to know you as you get to know him. Stay calm and patient, no matter the odds and provocation, but also be firm and ready to dispense mild discipline when needed. You'll be on your way to being a fine horseman.

AFTERWORD

In reading any book on horsemanship, it often seems as if the owning and using of a horse is filled with perils, seen and unseen, and has few joys to consider.

That's not true, as the number of horse owners in this country must show. But there are qualities of mind and skills of mind and body that are essential, as well as many special considerations. Unfortunately, in covering as many of the problems that could crop up with horses as possible it must sometimes seem to the reader as if those problems do crop up *all* the time.

Again, the truth of the matter is that even poorly treated horses sometimes amaze me with their resilience. But the properly cared for and trained horse can be so much better that the fact that someone would go to the trouble of having an improperly trained and cared for horse also amazes me.

To be a horseman, your horse must be properly trained and cared for, and horsemanship is the subject of this book, so much of it is devoted to those items.

As a matter of fact, the riding, which as I've said is a relatively small part of horsemanship, is just about one thing that cannot really be taught in a book. You must practice, and your practice will be much more valuable if it is done under the eye of an experienced horseman. If at all possible, your first hours in the saddle should be carried out with an instructor, whether paid or not, of great expertise. Nutrition, first aid, grooming proce-dures, general handling—anyone with a bit of sense, who can read, can learn about these. With, even here, a bit of practice. Riding is a different matter. The more time you spend on and with your horse, the more rapid will be your progress, both as a rider and as a horseman. Don't read a book and go out claim-ing to be an expert. Life works that way in only a few areas, so few that offhand I can't think of a single one.

Basically, learn to enjoy the time you spend with your horse. The horse will then learn to enjoy the time you're spending with it, and the entire relationship will be beneficial to both of you.

INDEX